HIKING the ROAD to RUINS

RIVERGATE REGIONALS

Rivergate Regionals is a collection of books published by Rutgers University Press focusing on New Jersey and the surrounding area. Since its founding in 1936, Rutgers University Press has been devoted to serving the people of New Jersey, and this collection solidifies that tradition. The books in the Rivergate Regionals Collection explore history, politics, nature and the environment, recreation, sports, health and medicine, and the arts. By incorporating the collection within the larger Rutgers University Press editorial program, the Rivergate Regionals Collection enhances our commitment to publishing the best books about our great state and the surrounding region.

HIKING the ROAD to RUINS

Day Trips and Camping Adventures to Iron Mines,
Old Military Sites, and Things Abandoned in the
New York City Area . . . and Beyond

SECOND EDITION,
Revised and Expanded

DAVID A. STEINBERG

RUTGERS
UNIVERSITY PRESS
New Brunswick, New Jersey, and London

Library of Congress Cataloging-in-Publication Data

Steinberg, David A.
Hiking the road to ruins : daytrips and camping adventures to iron mines, old military sites, and things abandoned in the New York City area—and beyond / David A. Steinberg.—Second edition, revised and expanded.
    pages cm.— (Rivergate regionals)
    ISBN 978-0-8135-6584-2 (paperback)—ISBN 978-0-8135-6586-6 (e-book)
    1. Hiking—New York (State) —Guidebooks. 2. Hiking—New York Region—Guidebooks. 3. Ruined buildings—New York (State) —Guidebooks. 4. Ruined buildings—New York Region—Guidebooks. 5. Abandoned mines—New York (State) —Guidebooks. 6. Abandoned mines—New York Region—Guidebooks. I. Title.

    GV191.42.N7S74 2015
    796.5109747--dc23
    2014017489

A British Cataloging-in-Publication record for this book is available from the British Library.
Copyright © 2015 by David A. Steinberg

Visit our website: http://rutgerspress.rutgers.edu

Manufactured in the United States of America

DEDICATION

This book is fondly dedicated to my family:
My son, Noah, and my lovely and patient wife, Emily, who
supported me throughout the long research and writing phases.

My parents, Phillip and Gloria Steinberg, who taught me to love
camping, hiking, the outdoors, and adventure. They taught by
example that all life is sacred. Dad would never kill any stray
insects that found their way into our home; he'd trap them and
carefully release them outside.
Bravo.

CONTENTS

INTRODUCTION

It isn't about the trees.

I do love to camp, hike, and explore with my camera, though. No matter how my body might ache, how distracted I might be with home or work issues, a good challenging day on the trail (looking for relics) resets me in a way nothing else will.

This second edition has been completely updated and revised. A few hikes from last time were removed (making them now neglected treks to abandoned ruins, something some might find too hard to resist), but for good reason: access problems, renovation, or anything else that makes the site unsuitable for our purposes. The new destinations will make this collection of hikes a lot of fun for those bold heroes who want an unusual day out but still might want to get home in time for dinner.

The best part about having published this book is that I've met many interesting fellow explorers of ruins or mines as a result. In many cases their knowledge of historic places and the lengths they'll go to in the name of exploration astounds me. Some are now friends who have invited me on some extraordinary expeditions. The fact that anyone had heard of this book or even actually *bought one* used to surprise me: I thought I was the only guy who cared about these kinds of things, but now I know the reality of the situation I've shoehorned myself into. I'm thankful I've made a connection with like-minded enthusiasts and grateful when anyone contacts me or shows up at one of my presentations.

A long time ago, I discovered that hiking to goals is more rewarding than just ambling around a circuit, and you might get some good pictures, too. Most trips are imagined as a series of smaller goals that eventually add up to something bigger (theoretically, when it all works out according to plan).

Be sure to take a lot of photos as you explore. Remote historic sites change from year to year, and rarely for the better. The old wooden buildings will eventually collapse or burn, some mine will fill in, or an old ghost town will get bulldozed. Get there while things are still standing and witness the sad magnificence some of these once-busy destinations present.

Within a relatively short drive of the New York metropolitan area there are a multitude of colorful abandoned sites worth seeking out. Ruins, iron mines or historic shelters (as an example) make especially fascinating goals for day trip adventures. Chapters are written as if you, the reader, are on one of my hikes, which I've always approached as guided tours. Historical iron mining, the Industrial Revolution, and the explosive population growth of the New York area have left us many opportunities for discoveries of ruins in forest settings, all within close proximity of the busiest city on earth. War is also very good for ruin hunters, as one obsolete military installation after another becomes legally available for exploration.

My goal is to put together a collection of good ideas for hikes and explorations to those places. I hope you find some information here that sparks your interest into finding out more: a perfect map, a book, a source that will encourage even further exploration to find some curious, mysterious, photogenic relic of our past.

I especially welcome fellow hike leaders of all sorts to these adventures. Even if you have never hiked a step, much less led a hike, anyone caught using this book is a de facto *hike leader,* an awesome responsibility and social promotion.

My site inclusion criteria for ruins, mines, and such are:
- It is within a two-hour drive of New York City (in most cases).

- It is on a clearly marked trail or identifiable woods road.
- It is legally accessible.
- It is photogenic.
- The hike itself is a pleasant nature experience.

SPECIAL NOTE TO HIKE LEADERS:
Because I've outlined the exact location of sites and listed most of the things I've come across, this book might take the thrill of discovery away from some people. For you, this is just another regrettable burden of the responsibility you'll unflinchingly shoulder as you lead your friends on hikes.

The motivation for my exploration has always been about photography. When I began seriously taking photos as a hobby, I would drag my friends all over the place in the name of good pictures. Fortunately, I know people who like to photograph as much as I do and are into the adventure. It wasn't long afterward that I started leading hikes for different organizations and began searching out interesting places to hike, looking for things and places that are visually stimulating and historically interesting.

I know that there is a twisted element of the population that enjoys accessing abandoned buildings, military leftovers, and the like, and not always legally. They are called Urban Explorers (they have plenty of self-congratulatory websites) and even do this odd activity in organized groups. Urban Explorers have their own noble code of ethics: do no damage to gain access; take nothing. They are not about B & E, and even less about law enforcement interface.

My affiliation with the elite IMF Photo Team, pioneers in high-concept urban exploration during the 1980s and 1990s, has previously not been known (up to the first edition, at least), but my work in the Research & Development Department at the IMF's New York office paved the way for me to begin chronicling the road to ruins. After some memorable missions the IMF became dormant as we grew up and stopped sneaking into places. Eventually the IMF was placed on inactive status, but the curiosity remained, and so years later the Road to Ruins Investigation Team became a logical extension of that secret investigative group in a quest to do it legally. Many former IMF Photo Team operatives have participated in Road to Ruins investigations.

I encourage a strict "leave no trace" ethic to these adventures. I would expect that removal of objects, introducing graffiti, making any kind of alteration, littering, or vandalism should be abhorrent to those with the interest to seek out these places. Leaders should be aware of how their hikers are behaving and shouldn't hesitate to intervene if needed, especially in regard to inexperienced participants or enthusiastic youngsters who aren't malicious at heart.

Know a good ruin somewhere? Infiltrate www.TheRoadToRuins.com with your tips or comments.

David A. Steinberg
Eastchester, NY
Summer 2014

PREPARATION

ITEMS TO BRING OR WEAR
Ankle-supportive hiking shoes, waterproof is a plus
Copy of the trail map, with the route highlighted and arrowed
FRS two-way radios
Fully charged cell phone
GPS receiver
Hand towel
Light-colored long pants
Sunglasses
Watch
Wicking clothing
Wide-brimmed hat

ITEMS TO PACK
Binoculars
Bug repellant
Camera, memory card, extra batteries
Compass (non-electronic)
First aid kit
Food and water, snacks
Original trail map
Paper
Pen

Plastic supermarket bags for trash
Rainwear
Reliable flashlight (bring two if you know you'll be inside a
mine or ruin)
Suntan lotion
Water filter
Whistle

MY FIRST AID KIT

Alcohol pads
Antibiotic ointment
Bandage tape
Band-Aids
Disposable lighter
Gauze
Itch relief pen (ammonia)
Moleskin (for blisters)
Pain reliever (small bottle of aspirin, acetaminophen, or ibupro-
fen with the cotton pressed in firmly to eliminate the rattling
noise while hiking)
Pepto-Bismol tablets
Pocket knife
Rubber gloves
Sewing kit (small, for minor repairs)
Tick pliers
Triangular bandage (sling)

SPEAKING THE LANGUAGE OF THE TRAIL

Blazes are colored markings that appear on rocks and trees. They
are the street signs of the trail. Each trail has its own color (or
design, or combination of colors). It is not unusual to have several
differently colored blazes sharing the same path. A single blaze of
one color means the trail continues straight ahead in the direction
you are going. Trail turns are indicated by two stacked blazes, with
the top blaze to the left or right of the blaze below. The trail turns
in the direction of the top blaze. A triangular configuration is the
beginning or end of the trail.

A **woods road** is an old dirt or gravel road used as a trail. It may be marked or unmarked.

A **cairn** (pronounced "carn") is a conspicuous pile of rocks that serves the same purpose as a blaze. There is no correct size. In these parts of New York and New Jersey they are usually placed on unmarked trails to point the way as you go. Sometimes they alert the hiker that an unmarked spur branches off to an overlook, mine, or other feature that is not on the trail proper. They are less formal than blazes and not generally placed by recognized trail maintainers.

Bushwhacking is leaving the known path and walking through trailless woods to get to a particular place.

Primitive campsites are typically remote tent sites. Staying at them requires survival planning.

The New York–New Jersey Trail Conference is the area's major recognized trail maintainer. In addition to clearing and blazing trails they print most of the hiking books and maps we use for reference and navigation, such as the *New York Walk Book,* frequently referred to as the *Walk Book.*

Abbreviations are commonly used when discussing trails. Fellow hikers you encounter on the way might ask how far ahead is the intersection where the AT (Appalachian Trail) crosses the LP (Long Path).

CELL PHONES

Annoying? Yes. Critical to have along? Yes.

As a leader, you should make sure that your hikers have your cell phone number keyed into their phones. This way, they can contact you if they get lost or injured (assuming service is available).

Chatting away on the trail is the height of clueless arrogance.

SAFETY

I do not advocate entering places that appear to be dangerous or are closed to the public, so use common sense at all times. Do not take any chances with your health or well-being, and think twice before taking foolish risks. Hike with a partner when you can.

I strongly suggest that you bring your properly stocked backpack with you everywhere you go at all times when hiking, even when entering places that look safe (such as iron mines that don't appear to be very deep, or somewhere that you think you'll only be in "for a minute"). How stupid would you feel if you twisted an ankle and your pack (with first aid) was just out of reach, or if a rock fall prevented an exit and your pack was on the other side of it? Don't take chances by dropping pack when your well-being might be at stake.

On these explorations you'll frequently be hiking on unmarked trails, exploring military remnants and inspecting deep iron mines. Before you go *anywhere,* give a detailed itinerary to someone (family, a park ranger, or leave a map on your desk at home), especially mentioning who you're with and when you expect to return. Photocopy the trail map twice and give one copy to someone at home with the intended route highlighted in yellow with arrows showing the direction of travel. You can also buy an extra copy of this book (it makes a great gift), thoughtfully give it to your contact, and tell them which chapter you're following. Always check in when you return. Use the other copy of the trail map to navigate while you keep the original safe and dry in your backpack.

Keep a full change of clothing (jacket or sweatshirt, footwear, underwear, socks, shirt and pants) in the car for your return. Extra food and water are also things that you'll be glad you stashed in the trunk. You should be prepared to deal with all sorts of surprises on these hikes.

FLASHLIGHT

Recent advances in LED flashlight technology have had the effect of providing inquisitive adventurers with strong, bright, power-efficient flashlights—the same batteries in a standard LED light will far outlast those in a Krypton incandescent light. LED bulbs also last for thousands of hours in many cases, far surpassing our old-style lights, but some (earlier or cheap ones) have a bluish cast and should be avoided. Krypton bulbs have largely gone the way of the dinosaurs and are not recommended for our explorations anymore, but if you have your beloved old-style torch and trust it, then go right ahead—but you should have more than one light with you, anyway. Super bright, quality-made Cree LED lights paired with either alkaline cells, rechargeable NiMH, lithium-ion, or non-rechargeable lithium cells are superior torches for our explorations, and even some inexpensive 9-bulb, 3-AAA cell "regular" LED lights are quite adequate, provided that the color is reasonably correct. I always carry at least one quality-made LED in my pack, loaded with alkaline cells, and another NiMH-loaded "go to" torch somewhere in a pocket or fanny pack, ready to serve as my main light. High-output Crees can drain batteries quickly, though.

About lumen ratings: this is largely subjective so don't take anyone's ratings as gospel. Generally, somewhere around 200 lumens ought to be more than enough for most purposes, taking light output versus power drain into consideration as well as effect on the eyes. Higher lumens = more power drain, resulting in shorter burn times per charge and higher heat output as well as being so bright they may be blinding in close quarters.

Plan to have enough light for two or three days in case something goes wrong, which means you should load some lights with rechargeable cells and others with alkaline cells because you should not rely on rechargeables alone. Headlights are also very useful to carry but can be somewhat limited for casual RTR explorations. They are, however, very good for camping trips. Always test your flashlights in a dark room the night before the trip.

Alkaline cells are a smart choice for affordable, reliable power. They put out 1.5 volts DC fully charged, hold the charge when unused, dim much more predictably than other types of power cells (thus, you know far in advance when it's time to change cells), and never die suddenly. You can leave new alkalines in your pack over time and feel secure that they'll perform when you install them. They are more expensive than "heavy duty" or "regular" cells and are heavier than rechargeable batteries. With any sort of battery, the output voltage will drop under load.

"(Super) Heavy Duty" cells are carbon, not alkaline, resulting in short burn times, so there's really very little "super" or "heavy duty" about them at all. Carbon cells from dollar-stores should be carefully scrutinized, because many are overseas knockoffs of well-known brands that are poorly manufactured, resulting in the very real possibility of a distressingly short charge or leaking acid that can damage your light. A major tip-off of cells to avoid is identifying spelling that's close to, but different from, well-known brands.

Lithium batteries last the longest and are considerably more expensive. Lithium-ion (Li-ion) rechargeables perform very well and have a long service span.

NiCad (nickel-cadmium) cells have a shorter burn time; an unfortunate recharge memory (if you recharge them before they're fully discharged, they'll never again charge up completely); and a sharp power use down-curve, which is not necessarily a bad thing, since they give almost full power output until they quit. They like to be discharged completely before recharging but have largely been replaced by NiMH cells.

NiMH (nickel–metal hydride) cells have a comparable life to NiCad and no recharge memory. They lose some of their charge when they aren't used (even those that claim not to), so if you use NiMHs or bring some as extras, you must recharge them every time you go out. When they're used up, the power drops off suddenly, like NiCads. For longer life, try to avoid discharging them completely and recharge as soon as possible.

NiCads or NiMHs are noticeably lighter to carry, and both put out 1.2 volts DC fully charged, meaning their light output may not be as intense as comparable alkaline cells.

Always bring spare batteries Never mix different battery types. Some devices, such as GPS, require you to set the device for the type of battery you're using.

MAPS

The personally rendered hand-drawn maps presented herein are not to scale and should be used for general location purposes only. I would not rely on them for navigation, and neither should you! Pick up the maps listed in the chapter introductions or online-search to supplement what you have.

Some maps, such as those put out by the New York–New Jersey Trail Conference, are exceptionally precise and updated every few years, reflecting trail relocations, new trails, and so on. They're also printed on tear proof/waterproof paper, making them last a very long time. Don't hang on to old maps. Update often and check websites for new information.

RESEARCH

Start from the top and work down: the National Park Service, National Forest Service, New York State Department of Environmental Conservation or state vacation guides/websites are great places to begin researching a trail. From there, write, call, or e-mail the park of your choice. Park rangers are the best source for specific answers to questions about campsites or trail conditions in their jurisdiction, and they can frequently tip you off to something interesting that isn't on the map.

Historical societies might sponsor hikes to old mines or historic sites of interest. Hiking clubs (Appalachian Mountain Club, Sierra Club, etc.) are valuable resources and orienteering clubs sometime produce excellent maps of trails. There are many excellent topo mapping programs using USGS quads: study those maps for indications such as ruins, caves, buildings (even where you "know" there aren't any!), and so on.

Some properties (such as Great Camp Santanoni) have a Unit Management Plan (UMP) that is available online. UMPs evaluate the site and include comprehensive inventories of all things natural and man-made within its border: very handy for us. Maps of points of interest are usually part of the report. Finally, keep your ears and eyes open for offhand references to anything along the lines of barely known primitive campsites, ruins, or historic sites.

ONLINE RESEARCH

I rarely print specific links because they can change at any time and you'll get better results doing fresh searches. Also, information can be dated or outright incorrect, so always corroborate by checking different sources against one that's known and trustworthy.

LEADING AND NOT LEADING HIKES

NOT LEADING A HIKE

Be prepared, because you are ultimately responsible for your own personal comfort and safety. Make sure you have the right gear and food, a trail map, and are behaving appropriately. If in doubt, be sure to ask questions before you go. The leader isn't your mother or father but will usually do anything possible to assure an enjoyable outing. After all, isn't that the idea?

Try to enjoy your time hiking through the peaceful green forest and over those bracing mountains. You aren't at work! Guiding people through the woods effectively isn't your problem, so let the leader lead. If you don't agree with the way things are going, rational discussion must displace anger in any debate. Questioning a decision on the leader's part is fine, but just because you don't agree doesn't mean someone is wrong. Heated arguing helps no one and turns the day sour. Most seasoned hike leaders should be confident enough in their abilities not to be threatened by a reasonable question or challenge. You might learn something from another point of view.

Given that the person leading the trip knows the route and how to get back (and very possibly has the car keys), it is in your interest to protect your leader, as the troops protect their general. This sounds severe and overstated for simple day hikes, and maybe it is, but the point is that if you cut off the head, the body dies.

LEADING A HIKE

Leading a hike successfully looks easy until you try it. When you imperiously set yourself up as a "hike leader," you pick the destination and research the history or natural features of the hike, secure the map, and make some copies for your friends, who may or may not know how to read it properly. You make sure your hikers are properly outfitted, decide how to get to the trailhead, select the trails you'll need to take, lead your hikers on the trail, find everything, assume responsibility for first aid, hope that the destination you've selected is worth the time investment (but you're in the woods, so how bad can it be, anyway?), and get them out safely, all the while enjoying the day. You must be strong and resourceful.

There is an assumption on the part of your hikers that you know what you're doing. Here's your opportunity to look like a genius by leading a hike that goes well and then enjoy all the gushing applause and cheers at the end. Unfortunately, you also open yourself up to criticism and disappointment when things don't go as planned. The margin of difference between a rousing success and a substandard failure can be slim.

Some quasi-military aphorisms become altogether fitting and proper:

- A plan is subject to change in the field.
- Hope for the best and prepare for the worst.
- Pressure makes diamonds.
- Good luck is the result of good planning. (I got that one from a fortune cookie.)

The underlying principle of all this is that it is important to plan ahead and have a reasonable strategy for the day's explorations. You'll need to be "liquid" and make changes as needed. Impossible water crossings or path-obstructing hazards might require you to alter the line of attack. Learn from your mistakes.

Putting your feet on the trail is the easy part of leading, but it's the people management aspects that are the real challenge! Be decisive. Waffling = indecision = weakness = your hikers won't trust you. Stick with the plan. "Firm but fair" is my guideline when leading groups. If you are the leader, it doesn't mean you are the sole decision-maker. Like the president, your hikers are your cabinet and you need to listen to them, but ultimate responsibility for the course of action is yours. You're the leader! Remember that if someone gets lost or hurt, it will be up to you to get that person to safety.

When leading a hike for a group, and assuming you are not being paid to perform these duties, you have a responsibility to protect those who have entrusted themselves to you. If you're getting paid, you also have a legal responsibility to supply the service you've been contracted to provide.

Some rules of thumb that may be helpful on the trail:

1. Count noses before the hike begins. Assign informal "buddies" or let participants pick their own. Do a head count at every rest stop.

2. Inform your hikers that if they lose the group, they should remain on the trail and stay put: soon enough, the leader will learn that they are not there and will backtrack in an attempt to find them. But if lost hikers have moved off the original route, the problems really begin.

3. When leading a group, tell the participants that they may hike at their own pace, but instruct them to always wait at any trail intersections, including those at unmarked trails or woods roads. They probably don't know the route you're taking that day, so they must stop. This also allows the group to come together, and some folks can rest while the others catch up.

4. Have your hikers inform you if they are feeling any pain at all. Meds in your first aid kit should be able to cope with anything from headaches and indigestion to forming blisters. You can only move as fast as your slowest hiker.

5. Hikers must notify you or their buddy when they are leaving the trail for bathroom breaks. Some clubs have informally scheduled "separations" where the men and the ladies split off.

6. FRS two-way transceivers are a good thing. Pick at least a 5-mile set, and once you appoint a "sweep" (the last person to follow the group on the hike) give that person the other radio and stay in touch. Make sure you get your radio back

after the hike! Put your name and phone number on it
somewhere.

7. Three of anything (fires, shirts), usually in a triangular
configuration, is the international distress signal. The
SOS is antiquated. If you are attempting to signal with
your flashlight, patterns of three dots with a suitable pause
between each set is standard.

8. Enthusiasm is contagious. If you're enjoying yourself and
having fun, your group will pick up on it. Your hike will
be a success, no matter what. If you're having a lousy day
and wish you were home watching the Mets game, they'll
pick up on that, too.

9. Respect the environment you're hiking through. Be sure
your hikers do no damage, don't litter, don't trespass on
private property, or throw rocks from high points, because
someone might be hiking below you.

EMERGENCY MEASURES

Red Cross First Aid Basics and CPR certifications are good things to
have before you begin hiking or leading groups. Another good thing
to have ready is a strategy for what to do when things go wrong.

Keep a cool head. If someone has a serious injury but it does
not prevent him or her from hiking, get to civilization/a road/a
ranger station/a home ASAP. This is not always possible, of course.
The important thing is to stay in control and be reassuring to your
charge. Keep encouraging the person to move forward, no matter
what, because the pain will persist whether help is found quickly or
not. The injured party needs to know that everyone will fare better
if he or she keeps moving toward proper medical care. Attempt to
make a cell phone call to 911, and inform rescue personnel where
you expect to emerge from the woods.

A far more critical situation arises if the injury prevents the
victim from walking. Not even a broken leg or sprained ankle will
prevent someone who is properly motivated from getting out of
the woods, but an unconscious person isn't going anywhere, and
carrying someone out is rarely the smart thing to do in that circum-
stance. Moving a wounded person is the last thing to be attempted

and could make the injury worse. Furthermore, it will slow down the move toward help if you're dragging an injured person along. You might have to leave the victim while you get help. It's a tough judgment call on the leader's part.

Make your injured hiker as comfortable as possible; mark his position on your map or with your GPS, and then leave to get help, possibly bringing someone with you. Have the others stay with the injured person. Do *not* send someone else with your map while you stay with the injured. As the leader, you alone know exactly where your hiker is, and you minimize the risk that your rescuer will get lost while frantically running through the woods. It might be smart to drop your heavy pack (but always carry water and a map with you) and move out as quickly as possible. This way, others can use your first aid kit, food, extra water, and clothing to comfort the victim. They might want to build a fire for warmth and signal purposes.

Basically, if you have a cell phone with good reception, just make the call and stay with the injured until assistance arrives. If it's just the two of you, leave the injured and get help as quickly as possible if there is no cell service available.

GETTING LOST

We all miss an intersection, bear left when the trail goes right, or lose the blaze. When it happens, maintain your grace under fire. Don't try to fix things by bushwhacking to where you think the trail is; instead, turn around and backtrack to the last blaze.

Once you are back at the last blaze, look around. In most cases, you should be able to see the next blaze on the trail you just came down. If no blaze is apparent, read the ground. Look for footprints or some sort of trail maintenance signs such as cut deadfall or a worn path. It is very rare that you'll see nothing. If that happens, leave the group at the last blaze and look around for an indication of where the trail is. If it's just two of you, keep each other in sight while you look for the trail, even if you have radio or phone contact. If the group is large enough, a few people can fan out and look for a sign (while others stay put), but they *must* keep the group within sight at all times. Getting lost and then losing your hikers while they helpfully wander off is completely *aggravating* and the worst situation outside of an injury that I know of. It shows a lack of control on the leader's part.

Hiking on unmarked trails is a whole different story. Many in the New York/New Jersey area are old woods roads that should be easy to follow, but if in doubt, follow the widest path and keep your map and compass handy. If you lose the trail, go back to the last place you are certain of and try again.

When all else fails and the bears are looking at you as if you're a giant salmon-blueberry burrito, follow water or a stream downhill, since streams almost always lead to civilization in some way. Whistling in repeated clusters of three toots is a good idea when trying to be located.

As you hike, be sure to pay attention to the blazes. Don't push on without seeing one, assuming you're on the trail. Trust your instincts, and if it feels wrong, there's a good chance it is.

AFTER THE HIKE

Leave a change of clothing in the car, including sneakers. A fresh shirt and pair of socks will make you feel human again after a long hike. A cooler with cold water and a snack is also good to reward yourself and friends with after a summer hike. In colder weather, a thermos full of hot chocolate or tea is like a gift from above. You'll be very glad you brought it.

USING GPS

In many chapters, I've included Universal Transverse Mercator (UTM) coordinates, useful for finding sites with Global Positioning System (GPS) receivers. I've only included codes for the harder to find sites; the others I've outlined should not be difficult to locate following my text. UTM is a digital version of the more traditional longitude/latitude system of location. The GPS code, in UTM, for the monument on Beacon Mountain is 18T 0588074 easting, 4593497 northing. On the receiver it looks like this: 18T 0588074, 4593497.

GPS is great at telling you where you are, but figuring out where you need to go takes time and practice. In most cases, the coordinates listed throughout the book were taken by me at each site. I've marked the waypoints, such as mountain peaks, mines, trail intersections, or other landmarks I want to remember when accuracy at the time was at least 19 feet or better. GPS is not always useful for a pinpoint location, but it will put you within a general area, and then it's up to you. Most GPS hand-held units use WGS84 (World Geological Survey of 1984) as their default map datum, though longitude/latitude is used instead of UTM. It should be easy to convert from longitude/latitude to UTM.

To use my coordinates, follow these steps:

1. Mark a current waypoint anywhere. It doesn't matter.

2. Highlight the UTM coordinates and change them to the
   new coordinates.
3. Change the name of the waypoint and even the identifying
   symbol.

It's like learning a new language. For an excellent tutorial on GPS
use, check out Garmin.com.

You can generate documentation of your hike by creating a
"track." At the trailhead, enable the "track" feature of your GPS,
which records an electronic "bread crumb" record of your adventure. Mark significant waypoints as you go. Stop the "track" at the
finish and save it, giving it any name you wish. The unit can then tell
you the total elevation changes and mileage. Transfer your new track
to a mapping program, and you can also transfer waypoints from the
mapping program to the GPS. That comes in handy when you want
to find something or have confusing territory to navigate through.

Using GPS to find sites or get out of being lost is a tremendous
advantage, but beware of staring down at the unit when there are
hazards in the area such as sudden drops, holes, mine shafts, or
impatient hiking partners.

If your GPS has an altimeter, always calibrate it at a known
value before you hike—that is, if your front steps are identified as
being at 200 feet above sea level (on a hiking map or USGS quad),
remember to check the altitude reading and make any corrections
before you go. Many GPS receivers read altitude and interpret it
barometrically, but as we all know, air pressures change constantly.
Paper maps are always correct in elevation values. Similarly, when
you change batteries in the unit, you must recalibrate the compass.

The GPS is not a substitute for a paper map. I use the Garmin
Etrex Vista, which allows me about twelve hours of battery time for
my walk.

1
THE ARMY TUNNELS

WHERE: Tackamack Town Park and Blauvelt State Park, NY
WHY: Long tunnels and other structures from a former rifle range
DIFFICULTY: Easy; about 4 miles round-trip, with minimal elevation changes
MAP: None available that is accurate (except for mine)
DIRECTIONS: New York State Thruway (I-87) north over the Tappan Zee Bridge, and take the first exit on the other side, Route 9W south. Go about a half-mile south and turn right (west) on Route 28, Old Mountain Road. Continue on 28 (now Clausland Mountain Road) to the parking lot for Tackamack County Park, on the right

Known locally to dope-smoking, sex-crazed teenagers as the "Army Tunnels," these odd passages through the woods are actually the remains of Camp Bluefields, a National Guard rifle range from the 1910s.

Camp Bluefields was built by the National Guard in 1910 as a replacement for its range at Creedmoor, NY. It also served as a World War I POW camp, according to the Army War College. As a shooting range, no one ever seemed to be happy with the site. Marksmen complained about shooting at targets with the sun in their eyes, and locals were upset when errant bullets overshooting the mark wound up piercing their homes. By 1912, the Guard ceased its operations. Between 1913 and 1918, the YWCA used the land as a summer camp for working New York City women. In

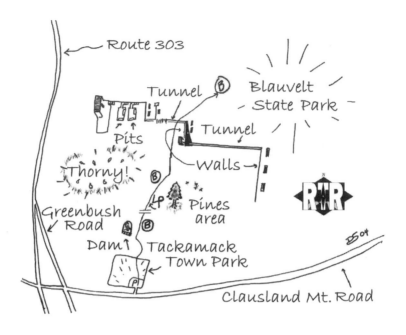

later years, it was an ROTC training camp and was then used by soldiers from nearby Camp Shanks (a major East Coast departure point for troops going to the European theater during World War II) for training. Camp Bluefields was abandoned soon after the war, left alone in the woods to endure the uncaring ravages of the elements and bored youth.

This particular adventure is more of an exploration than a true hike, since we'll be on only one trail (the blue Long Path) going and coming. The distance isn't that great. What takes all the time is poking our noses into the nooks and crannies associated with the site. So what are we waiting for?

The only "official" map of the area that I was able to find was the New York–New Jersey Trail Conference map for the Palisades, on which the Long Path is featured as it passes through Blauvelt (pronounced "Blawvelt," Dutch for "bluefield") State Park. The problem is that the features we're interested in aren't depicted on the map. The village of Orangetown has a parks department at 81 Hunt Road that was very helpful in my quest for maps and information on this park and also on Clausland Mountain County Park, an old Nike base nearby. The hand-drawn map they gave me had good, general, lay-of-the-land information, but the rifle range isn't accurately represented, and the location of the trails shown is also a question mark. Fortunately, we really don't need a trail map because the Long Path goes right to the middle of the site. You'll want to be sure to bring your Big Flashlight on this trip.

Okay then. From the parking lot, we'll pick up the blue Long Path and follow it (north) through the woods. The park, and likewise Clausland Mountain Park to the south, is named for Jan Claus, or Tackamack, the "clever Indian." He was an early landowner in Rockland County who sometimes acted as an agent in land deals with Dutch settlers. The trail skirts an old dammed pond and then passes through a low, muddy area alongside a stream. Crossing a road by some new development, the trail ascends to a stand of evergreens.

We feel that familiar "ruin sense" tingle when the trail suddenly comes upon a low wall and crosses over it. Of course, we'll leave the LP at this point and begin our investigation. This concrete "road"

we're following to the right (east) is actually the roof of the first tunnel we'll find today. The entrance is at the end of the "wall" and easily located. Pulling out our flashlights, we can enter and walk the few hundred feet through to a point where it is collapsed and flooded. Beer cans and alienated teenager graffiti line the passage. As the introduction of things to come, it's exciting to explore. After turning

Dave on the tunnel roof.
Photo by Todd Rutt.

around at the collapse, exit, and then continue to the right, following along the wall. There are recesses and electrical tubing in the wall.

The targets were on two rails that were raised above the wall. After the rifleman shot at the target, it was lowered so a marker could be placed in the bullet hole, and then it was lifted back up. The rifleman could then see where his round went and take another shot.

Things get interesting quickly around here. Passing some empty blockhouses, we'll hop up onto the ledge to our right and follow it to the end. Suddenly, we're pretty high up. An opening we come across shows where a stairway used to descend to the depths of the "tower." The litter at the bottom suggests there must be an easy way down there, but how? We'll retrace our steps to where we can hop off the ledge and walk down to the base of the structure, passing a somewhat large hole in the wall along the way. No way are we climbing through there, even in the name of exploration. We do have our limits, after all . . . right?

There's another wall straight ahead which we now recognize as the roof of another long tunnel. We'll follow alongside it and as soon as possible scramble gracefully to the top and walk along the length,

Army tunnel entrance

passing various leftover artifacts on the ground as we go. Making our way to the end, we know the entrance to the tunnel beneath us must be here. Before we find and enter it, let's follow our last wall as it heads off to the right, passing some more blockhouses. It seems someone has attempted to make a cozy cabin of the last one.

It's now time to turn around, enter the long tunnel and follow it back through the semi-darkness to the far opening. The tunnels all have narrow window slits that allow in light and air. Surprise! We've wound up inside the base of the tower, amid the seemingly endless beer cans. What now? Explore the rooms, and yes, climb out through the hole we refused to enter just a little bit before, into the sunlight. A strange little circuit, for sure.

Retracing our steps from before, let's head back toward the first tunnel. We know we can't go through it to the end, so we'll trace it from the outside past the collapsed section, crossing back over the LP along the way. Within a short time another wall branches off to the right with two additional blockhouses standing guard. It doesn't go far and there isn't anything new in that direction, but we can go and check it out.

Mark escapes from the tunnel

Right at that point, the tunnel opens again beneath the roots of a tree. Ducking down, we'll enter and follow it through the semi-darkness. Deep cracks run along the middle of the walls of both sides of the tunnel, and the roof leans drunkenly. This section is obviously about to collapse at any moment, and if we judge it so, we shouldn't enter. At the exit, the thorn bushes, which have been only nuisances up to now, become more problematic. Hugging the wall and doing our best to keep the blood inside our veins, let us make our way to the next corner, where more surprises await. Making the left turn, two sets of crumbling stairways tunneling under the wall appear a few yards down. Upon closer inspection, we see they lead to some sort of closed-ended pits with walls and blockhouses. We'll dutifully explore the pits and then climb back out, continuing the search forward.

At the end of the wall, at the corner, decrepit stairs lead up to a two-story structure (one level is below the one we see) whose door has been cruelly ripped from the jamb and lies buried nearby under leaves and dirt. An anticlimactic conclusion to our explorations, but that's the way it goes sometime. This is the end of the line. As explorers, we do hate to turn around and retrace our steps back to the LP for exit, but those thick stands of thorn bushes will prevent us from bushwhacking back to the trail we came in on. I know this for a fact, since the RTR Investigation Team wound up bloody trying to find another exit.

I won't bore anyone with the endless stories of Satanism or ghostly haunted blockhouses that seem to follow places like this around. Haunted spots in the woods and empties go hand-in-hand for some odd reason. Just what *is* the connection between beer and Beelzebub? You have to work hard to attach anything evil to this place. The Army Tunnels are a fascinating and unique historic site that are worthy of our attention.

2
BEACON MOUNTAIN CASINO

WHERE: Beacon, NY

WHY: Reservoir and dam ruins, abandoned fire tower, casino and inclined plane railway remains, little-seen Daughters of the American Revolution (DAR) monument, high Hudson River viewpoints

DIFFICULTY: Challenging; about 9 miles round-trip, with moderate to steep climbs and one summit scramble

MAP: New York–New Jersey Trail Conference Map, East Hudson Trails

UTM COORDINATES: DAR monument: 18 T 0588074, 4593497

DIRECTIONS: Taconic State Parkway north to Route 301 west, toward Cold Spring. At the intersection of 301 and 9D, turn right (north). Go about 2 miles past the parking area for Breakneck Ridge (once through the tunnel) and look for blue blazes on a telephone pole, just past a private home (about 4 miles from the intersection of Route 301). The parking area is just north of the blazed pole, on the left side of the road, about 2 miles south of the town of Beacon on Route 9D

It's true that this particular outing may be shorter on things abandoned than some of the other hikes in this book, but the quality of the points of interest is high, sometimes literally. Additionally, Beacon Mountain and its twin summits are definitely less visited than the other peaks in this mountainous chain of the Hudson Highlands, thus fewer encounters with other humans could be listed in good conscience as another "why." Did I mention it's also an extremely attractive setting for a day's exploration? I just did.

Beginning on the blue-blazed Notch Trail (we've also taken it on the Breakneck Ridge hike), we pass by the remains of an old

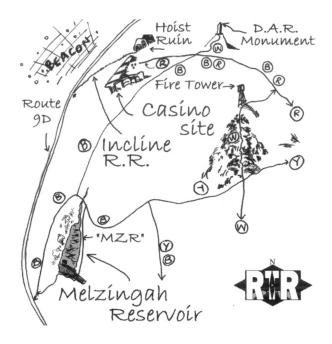

reservoir system on the way up. Keep all this plumbing in mind; we'll explore the system that supported it later in the day. Continue climbing on a gradual but steady uphill incline to a point where an unmarked woods road comes in to meet us, at 1.4 miles from the beginning. Again, make a mental note of the spot for later. It will all come full circle.

Stay to the right. Blazes are sometimes far apart in this section, and these woods roads can lead to confusion for those hikers who are not as clear-thinking as we are. Blue always goes uphill, sometimes more steeply, and at 2.2 miles another unmarked woods road appears with trees mysteriously marked "MZR" in yellow paint. Keep this point in mind for . . . oh, never mind. This trail heads down to the Melzingah Reservoir, which we'll explore on the way back. For now stay on blue until the yellow Wilkinson Memorial Trail joins up, named for trail builder Samuel L. Wilkinson. We part with blue and pick up yellow, still heading north. Painted rocks point out the way to "FT," or "Fire Tower" in this area. We're at about 800 feet in elevation.

Another intersection of trails comes in at 0.6 mile from the last one, along with yet another unmarked road, which disappears into the woods on a bearing toward private property. The white-blazed Breakneck Ridge Trail makes an appearance here, on the way to its terminus on South Beacon Mountain. White/yellow travel northward together for a short time until a cairn marks the spot where white cuts to the left and goes sharply uphill and yellow continues straight. Of course, we follow the white trail as it climbs to about 1,300 feet, finally giving us our first viewpoints over to the Hudson River and the Melzingah Reservoir, which is between us and the river. If binoculars are available, look down at the structure on the far side of the reservoir. Some sort of building. Hmmm . . .

The Schofield Ridge, which also includes Breakneck Ridge, is to our southeast, and Mount Taurus pokes its head up just behind it. The work begins again with a series of scrambles and climbs to the summit of South Beacon Mountain. The fire tower comes into view on the right as we climb, and once we level off, the tower is just ahead. While we lunch by the tower at 1,610 feet, let's take in the view. Dennings Point is the peninsula straight ahead in the Hudson. The city of Beacon is below us, and the New-burgh-Beacon Bridge stretches across the river. Speaking of New-burgh, that's it, directly across the Hudson from

Fire tower

us. The casino site is at the bare patch hanging on the western end of the ledge across the valley from us, near the radio towers. To the north and west we can spy the Shawangunk, Catskill, and occasionally Adirondack Mountain chains on a clear day.

The fire tower is unsafe to climb, though a restoration project is currently under way. Common sense, even for us intrepid ruins-hunters, will take over quickly if a climb is attempted. There are signs:

TOWER CLOSED TO PUBLIC

WARNING
DANGEROUS STRUCTURE
PLEASE KEEP CLEAR
N.Y.S. Department of Environmental Conservation
Albany, New York 12233

Mysterious blue blazes and arrows suddenly appear along with white as we make our way (still north) down from South Beacon, heading toward the casino. We do our best to follow the white blazes on the way down, but the markings come and go. If we just head downhill, we'll be fine.

At the bottom, more blue and red markings appear. This is one rare instance where these trails do not appear on the New York–New Jersey Trail Conference map, but the *Walk Book* map has the red trail. Let's follow to the left (northwest) and trust our judgment as we stay on the "main" trail, now a woods road. Red heads out (in a fashion) toward the casino site, and blue heads the same way but then abruptly diverts to the left (south) and drops down. Watch for the place where blue turns and descends, because that's our exit later, but it also marks where we begin to look for the trail to the elusive and dimly remembered Daughters of the Revolution monument.

When blue turns, stay on the road. Take the first right turn going uphill toward the communication towers. There are a few roads going toward the towers, and it doesn't matter which one we take. At the towers, turn right and continue uphill. The first left will take us to another group of radio towers, and sporadic white blazes are present in the area but can be difficult to spot if we aren't paying attention. The white blazes follow a radio tower installation fence to the summit of North Beacon Mountain, which actually is one mountain with a split summit. Following the fence will bring us to the DAR Memorial obelisk (near 18T 0588074, 4593497).

The 27-foot obelisk, erected on July 4, 1900, commemorates the burning of signal fires on the top of the mountain during the American Revolution. It stands on top of North Beacon Mountain, overlooking the city. From his headquarters in Newburgh, General Washington must have had a nice, clear view of the fires. At one time the monument was a highlight of trips to the top, along with the casino, but these days it is dwarfed by the communication towers up there and is virtually impossible to spot from below. I get the feeling that *no one* comes up here anymore except for Daughters of the American Revolution and history enthusiasts. It isn't marked on any map that I've seen of the area. The elevation is about 1,531 feet, higher than either Breakneck Ridge or Mount Taurus.

After a short break, returning downhill to the red trail will bring us back on the road to the casino ruins. (Past editions of the *Walk Book* mention ruins of summer cottages on this road, but they are actually on the northern/eastern side of the mountain, above the casino site. I haven't been there recently, and my informants have told me that they have fallen apart.) The site of the

Casino site

casino will come up shortly. An incline funicular (fyoo-NIK-yoo-ler, *adj.:* worked by a rope or cable) railway brought visitors 1,200 feet up to the casino, a lateral distance of 2,200 feet.

The casino site overlooks Beacon and gives scenic high views of the Hudson Valley. We've seen this particular panorama from the top of South Beacon Mountain. Exploring the site, we'll find stone walls with various openings, terraced areas of concrete slab that are decaying and broken, and foundations that suggest magnificent edifices. Crumbling steps to vanished structures are in a few different places. A broken ladder to a long-gone observation platform, rusted and neglected over the passing years, stands unusable behind the hoist house. Feel free to test your nerve, but three steps are quite enough to prove this might be a good way to end the hike in an unhappy way. The fire tower from before is visible up on South Beacon Mountain, behind us. There is enough here to keep us happily exploring for an hour. Multitudes of different radio towers overlook the scene, intrusive newcomers to this formerly grand destination.

The Mohawk Construction Company built the incline railway in 1902, and the Otis Elevator Company contributed the machinery. Two 33-foot-long cars ran in opposite directions on a single track at a speed of 500 feet per minute with a turnout at the halfway point. A hoist assisted the cars on the way up. The casino was built at the top in

Incline railroad cables

1902 and operated until a fire destroyed it in 1927. A hotel was built next to the casino in 1908, but fire also terminated that establishment in 1932. The last passengers went up the incline in 1978, but yet another fire in 1983 finally ended the operation.

The ruin of the cable hoist house is a prominent feature of the casino site and is unmistakable. After completing our investigation and taking pictures, it's time to start our descent, but there's still a little more to see before we're done.

Take the blue trail as it drops down, down, twisting our ankles and crossing streams before finally meeting up with . . . the blue trail! Intersection of blue and blue. It isn't hard to understand why we only see the blue blazes as we're coming down. This is an unfortunate choice of colors for the newly blazed descending trail, and someone should change it to green immediately, paint the trees on both sides, and mark it on a map. The blue trail we meet is the same Notch Trail we came up on. Remember the unmarked woods road I told you to keep in mind earlier? This is it.

We could take the Notch Trail straight back to the car, but we won't. Instead, we'll bear left (northeast) on the Notch and retrace our steps to the unmarked "MZR" (for Melzingah Reservoir) woods road we passed earlier on. Yes, it's all coming together very nicely right now. Take the trail to the right (southwest), and soon the trail splits. If we go left, the trail crosses the brook and continues on the road, using the path of least resistance. Of course, we'll bear right and follow the trail to a spot where it dead-ends at a brook crossing near a footbridge that is now gone, except for the two steel rails that held planks at one time. It isn't hard to cross over somewhere else and then rejoin the old road as it heads down to the reservoir.

The final RTR exploration site for today is the Melzingah Reservoir, still serving the city of Beacon. A small but imposing concrete dam holds firm, and we can now get a closer view of that square building we spotted earlier. Turning around, we look up the mountain to see if we can locate that vantage point. Were we really that high up?

There are a few dirt roads around the dam. Head over to our right (to the northern or far side of the dam), and there is a foot trail that we can pick up after hopping down to the spillway. It is plainly visible when you're there. Following the path brings us to another smaller reservoir with broken dam structures and two pump houses, one on either side of the brook. This path leads back to the blue Notch Trail and our vehicle. The reservoir system now makes more sense to us as we retrace the blue trail downhill, past features we remember from much earlier today.

This adventure really had a nice variety of exploration opportunities. I've always liked that DAR monument in particular because I believe not many people know about it or venture way up there to find it if they do. Some people might ask, "Who cares?" I'd say, "People who buy books pointing out abandoned towns or iron mines might."

3
THE BOSTON HARBOR ISLANDS

WHERE: Various-sized islands scattered throughout Boston Harbor
WHY: Extensive collection of military forts and other ruins
DIFFICULTY: Easy; negligible walking on each island, reached by water shuttle
MAP: National Park map
BOOK: *All About the Boston Harbor Islands* by David and Emily Kales
WEBSITES: www.bostonislands.com, www.nps.gov/boha/index.htm
CONTACT: 617-223-8666
DIRECTIONS: See text

The Boston Harbor Islands National Recreation Area offers the curious traveler a unique opportunity for discovery because a surprisingly large number of people, even from the area, know nothing of these islands. There are enough ruins and military leftovers to keep us contentedly exploring for many days, requiring frequent-as-possible repeated visits. Fortunately, we can maximize our experience by carefully taking advantage of the reservable primitive campsites that are on several of the islands, notably Bumpkin, Grape, Lovell's, or Peddock's. If you're exploring the islands with me, we're definitely going camping! I'm only discussing islands that are currently served by the ferry, although virtually every island in the harbor has a ruin or structure of some sort. Some recently reopened islands offer swimming, hiking, or other recreation.

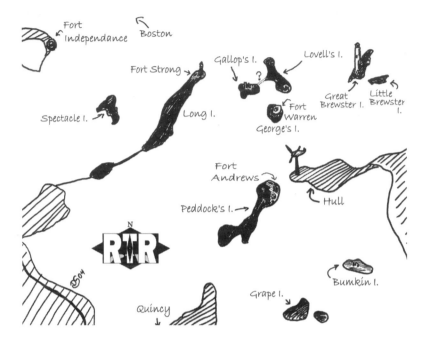

Access to the islands is by public or private ferries, and an additional ferry runs between the outer islands, using George's Island as a hub. You pay your fare at the mainland docks but ride for free between islands. In a pinch, you can hire one of the water taxis headquartered in Boston to take you out to the islands, but that's expensive. You can use your own boat to explore the harbor, if you have one.

It's generally recommended that you don't try to see more than two islands per day, which is why camping is such a good idea; exploring your own private island after the crowds go home is quite a good way to satisfy your curiosity. The idiosyncratic ferry schedule also makes going back and forth between the islands more of a problem than you'd expect it to be, so my advice is to keep it simple and not be over-ambitious in your explorations.

The close proximity of Logan Airport, one of the nation's busiest, should be noted since these islands can be pretty noisy during the day because of the incessant air traffic. As the big jets are coming in to land, they're low and loud, and at times you can clearly see the people inside. It does get better at night, but you sure do feel as if you're camping on the end of the runway sometimes.

Two crucial informational resources are the main islands' phone number, 617-223-8666, and the above-listed websites. Research every aspect of the trip before you go. Never assume anything when making plans to visit the islands, because ferry schedules or available campsites can change from year to year and even day to day. Check the website for an up-to-date ferry schedule, and it is a good idea to call the main information number for confirmation.

There are different options for formulating our plan of attack, so let's go over them:

OPTION #1: The most obvious choice is to pick up the ferry from Long Wharf in downtown Boston directly to George's Island and then pick up one of the free ferries that go to the other islands. The big negatives for this option are the expense of garaging the car downtown (figure on about $100 for two days) and dealing with nightmarish Boston traffic.

OPTION #2: Pick up the ferry from either Quincy Shipyard or Hingham Shipyard, depending on which one is in use at the time, on the south shore of the harbor. Parking is free in Quincy or Hingham Shipyard. You can save significant time by going directly to your campsite on one of the outer islands first instead of changing boats at George's, and there's no maddening city traffic to deal with either. This is a very good option.

OPTION #3: Pick up the ferry from Hull at the eastern end of the harbor. It's a longer drive to the dock but a shorter ride to some of the islands. (Peddock's is only about a quarter-mile from Hull.) Free parking is available near the ferry slip. This is another good option. It's also kind of neat to check out that huge wind turbine at the Coast Guard station that looks like it's about to cleave your skull in half.

OPTION #4: Take Amtrak from Penn Station to Boston (the high-speed Acela is an expensive but compelling thought), walk or taxi the short distance to Long Wharf, jump on the boat to George's, and then take a shuttle to your island of choice.

Before we begin, a primer on the five major eras of fort building in the United States is in order:

First System: 1794–1807

Second System: 1807–1817
Third System: 1817–1876 (*Most of our ruins come from this era.*)
Endicott System: 1890–1920 (*World War I is in this time frame.*)
World War II era: late 1930s–1945

GEORGE'S ISLAND

The main tourist destination and ferry hub (all boats go there), George's is the only island with dependable drinking water and food service available. Started in 1833, imposing Fort Warren took twenty years to complete under the supervision of West Point's Sylvanus Thayer. Arched labyrinths weave up, down, and through the fort on different levels, similar to the other big Third System island forts we've seen everywhere from Pea Patch Island (Fort Delaware) to the Florida Keys (Fort Jefferson). There is easily an afternoon's worth of exploring to do here, and if you're in luck you might spot the Lady in Black, the resident ghost.

The fort has been restored in recent years, and tours are usually offered during the summer season. As you're exploring the islands, at some point you'll wind up on George's Island.

Don't count on the island's food service or water availability for survival if you're camping. It's just not set up to supply you, so bring your own.

In recent years, the Boston Harbor Association has sponsored free guided trips to George's on the second Thursday of July and August.

PEDDOCK'S ISLAND

This is one of the largest of the islands, with a concentration of Endicott-era and World War II ruins and batteries from old Fort Andrew on the northern end. For us dyed-in-the-wool ruin hunters, this is the real deal, and we don't even have to sneak in! When we explore by the last light of day, the old gun emplacements stare balefully out at us from under their landscaped camouflage.

The campsites are on an open field close to the dock, and a water spigot fed from the mainland is onsite. In my experience the water is usually "on," but I wouldn't count on that for my camping needs. On my last visit during late summer 2011 the campsite was surprisingly crowded, and privacy was nearly nonexistent. There is plenty

Peddock's Island

to see, though, so pitch here and visit another island but save the investigation of this one for after 5:00 P.M., when the ferries stop running and the crowds disappear. Do you have the nerve to explore the old batteries by flashlight after dark?

LOVELL'S ISLAND
More excellent Endicott and World War II military ruin hunting is featured here. I have nothing against restoration, but you just can't beat some nicely photogenic decay.

Gun batteries from Fort Standish are at the island's north and south tips, with more to discover in the middle. Centrally located Battery Burbeck-Morris is the location, in my opinion, of the entrance to the fabled tunnel between this and Gallop's Island. The most popular description of the tunnel entrance refers to a studded door at the bottom of a ladder going uphill. This would be at the first battery we come to when approaching from the south, though the door is now cemented closed.

As we walk the beach we'll discover the collapsed Protected Switchboard Room, once used for furtive communications during

Battery Terrill

Inside a Lovell's Island ruin

Exploring an encasement

Inspecting a doorway on Lovell's Island

World War II but now only a pancaked pile of debris, difficult to identify. Early exploration can be rewarding, since Battery Terrill at the north tip is especially spooky in early morning light. Return to your campsite after the shuttles stop running, and take the time to explore this island in detail.

A cart at the dock is available for getting gear to the campsite. The choice sites are #6 and #7 at the end of the beach and a long walk from the dock. Site #7 is the best, being large and boasting a fine view of the harbor and the sparkly Deer Island waste water treatment plant. Campsite #6 next door is smaller, doesn't have close beach access or the view that #7 has but at least it's somewhat near the water. The other sites are small, located further inland without any water views and are tolerable camping at best.

BUMPKIN ISLAND
The only non-military ruins accessible by ferry are here. What's left of the old hospital for paraplegic children awaits our attention at the island's high point on the middle trail; however most of the

structure has collapsed into heaps of brick and tile. The hospital was opened by a philanthropist and was used from 1900 to World War I. A fire in 1945 destroyed most of the building, leaving just the shell until that, too, came down. The trail to the lookout passes two sets of foundations, one massive, that we'll properly inspect after we set up camp.

The four isolated campsites on the water are the best reservable campsites in the islands: wooded, level, on the beach, and bugs are not an issue. There are additional inland sites that are also pleasant. It's another long walk to the sites from the dock, but there is a cart here also.

LITTLE BREWSTER ISLAND
The historic Boston Light is on Little Brewster Island. Special three-and-one-half-hour excursions from Boston go out there to tour the light, which can be climbed.

GRAPE ISLAND
Short hiking trails and a few pleasant but unremarkable campsites are here for your entertainment. Wild edible berries abound. This is one of the few islands with no man-made structures to see.

CASTLE ISLAND
Now connected to the mainland by landfill, Castle Island's foremost claim to fame is that Edgar Allan Poe served there at Fort Independence (built under the Second System and upgraded under the Third System) in 1827 as a young man. The legend of an incident around 1817 involving a duel between two soldiers caught his attention, mainly because the unpopular victor wound up being sealed behind a wall under construction. Poe wrote his story "The Cask of Amontillado" based on the tale. The fort's many rooms are currently in use by the local community; it has only one level and is in distressingly good condition.

4
THE C & O CANAL

WHERE: Washington, DC, to Cumberland, MD

WHY: Mill ruins, aqueducts, lift lock remains, caves, huge tunnel, primitive campsites, Civil War–related sites

DIFFICULTY: Challenging; 184.5 miles, with a 600-foot elevation change in 8-foot (average) steps

BOOKS: Towpath Guide to the C & O Canal by Thomas F. Hahn (Harpers Ferry Historical Association), The C & O Canal Companion by Mike High (Johns Hopkins University Press), 184 Miles to Adventure (Boy Scouts of America)

WEBSITES: www.nps.gov/choh, www.Bikewashington.org/canal

CONTACT: C & O Canal National Historical Park, P.O. Box 4, Sharpsburg, MD 21782; phone 301-739-4200

VISITORS CENTERS: Georgetown: 1057 Thomas Jefferson Street, NW, Washington, DC 20007; phone 202-653-5190

Great Falls Tavern: 11710 MacArthur Boulevard, Potomac, MD 20854; phone 301-767-3714

Brunswick: 40 West Potomac Street, Brunswick, MD 21716; phone 301-834-7100

Williamsport: 205 West Potomac Street, Williamsport, MD 21795; phone 301-582-0813

Hancock: 326 East Main Street, Hancock, MD 21750; phone 301-678-5463

Western Maryland Station: Room 304, 13 Canal Street, Cumberland, MD 21502; phone 301-722-8226

Unique historic sites and prime primitive campsites make the venerable C & O a worthy destination. The Chesapeake & Ohio barge canal,

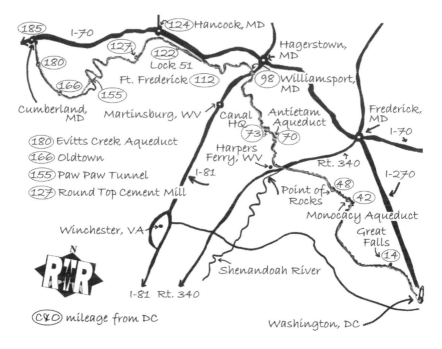

in use from 1829 to 1924, runs over 184 miles along the Potomac River from Washington, DC, to Cumberland, MD. After almost a hundred years of use, floods and changing technology (especially railroads) forced it out of business. It became a national historic park in 1971. There is so much to see along the trail that a detailed breakdown is impractical for this book. Instead, I've outlined some highlights.

My favorite places along the canal:

1. Monocacy Aqueduct
2. Harpers Ferry, WV
3. Caves around the halfway point
4. Dam #5 and the crossover area just north of the dam
5. Lock #46
6. Fort Frederick State Park
7. Round Top Cement Mill
8. Paw Paw Tunnel

The first thing to do is to consider some logistics. Hiking the canal at an average of 10 to 15 miles per day means that about three weeks

or so are required to do the trip, figuring in a rest day (or area exploration) or two. Biking it takes half the time. The canal towpath is
level, except for eight-foot average rises at the lift locks. The condition of the path is usually dirt or gravel, but it can get "rooty" and
rock-strewn as we move further west, and mud is always an issue.
The elevation of terrain is higher at Cumberland (about 620 feet)
and drops as we head toward DC, so it makes perfect sense to hike
or bike it in that direction. Most of the tour books, however, start
out at DC and tick off the miles heading west and so, for the sake of
continuity, we'll do the same.

Biking is really the best way to explore the entire length of the
canal in a reasonable amount of time and gives you more flexibility
as to where you stay. Although plausible, backpacking 26 miles to
our first campsite is also a tough nut, so for my mental health we'll
do it this way.

Whether we're doing the entire 184 miles or breaking it up into
bite-sized one-way chunks, getting back to the starting point is
our primary challenge, unless we are doing an out-and-back loop.
Major cities along the route are Washington, DC; Harper's Ferry,
WV; Hagerstown, MD; Martinsburg, WV; and Cumberland, MD.
Amtrak (trains 29 and 30) or Greyhound serves all of them, but
check websites for exact information. A private car shuttle from one
of the bike shops along the route will cost about a dollar a mile, and
some places will charge you for their return trip.

Making an arrangement with a shuttle service can be good, especially when you're only doing smaller pieces. Leave your car at the
end point of the trail, and have the shuttle bring you and your gear
to the beginning of the ride. Then you bike to your car.

If public transportation is used, leave your gear at the trailhead
or hotel room (or leave your partner with the stuff at one of the
hiker/biker campsites), drive your car to the end point, then take the
bus or train back to the beginning to start the trip.

Taking bikes and gear onto the train in Cumberland is a problem
because there are no checked luggage facilities there, and they won't
let you do it yourself. Greyhound accepts boxed bikes, but there may
be a surcharge if weight restrictions are exceeded. Don't plan to go
one-way by bike and expect to return by public transportation.

The park service information packet has campground details, camping regulations, bicycling advice and repair shops, canoeing information, boat ramp inventory, recreational facilities, and river access points to the hiker/biker/overnighter campsites (for those canoeing the Potomac). They can also advise regarding towpath washouts or relocations. Floods and hurricanes have damaged the canal in the past, requiring some adjustments to the route.

Do not even consider doing the trip without a towpath guide. The different guides all have something to offer:

- *Towpath Guide to the C & O Canal* offers a complete inventory of canal structures and histories.
- *The C & O Canal Companion* gives better traveling advice than the other books.
- *184 Miles to Adventure* is a no-nonsense travelogue with good maps.

Campsites are spread out at about 6-mile intervals throughout the route, making our exploration one big, exciting camping trip. Some campsites are called "hiker/biker overnighters" (H/B/O), meaning that they are reachable only via the towpath. Stays are limited to one night. A few are car accessible, making supply drops or exits convenient. There is water (seasonal, usually turned on around April 10) at the campsites, as well as picnic tables, outhouses, and fire rings. Several sites are very close to the river, making them pleasant places to stay. Locals favor the sites closest to town. Beware of poison ivy.

The first H/B/O is at Swain's Lock, 16 miles down, so we have our work cut out for us. Unfortunately, since it is the first campsite, it can fill early (or even be closed), so we need to be mentally prepared to go on to the next site, Horsepen Branch, at mile 26.1. Before we begin thinking about starting a little further down, understand that the first bunch of miles are interesting and worth the trouble. It's one of the few watered sections of the canal we'll encounter.

Noted miles from DC are approximate.

0: Starting out from Georgetown, the towpath calmly winds through the nation's capital as it passes by apartment buildings and stores (and the Watergate) before hitting the first of the

seventy-four lift locks on the trip. We also pass under several highway bridges we'd probably recognize more easily from topside.
There are fourteen locks in the first 10 miles of the ride. Note how
they all "rise." There is a reason saner people do the trail in the
opposite direction.

14: The Great Falls of the Potomac come in. George Washington's 1785 Potowmack Canal remains are on the Virginia side,
an early attempt to skirt the treacherous falls of the river for car-
go-bearing vessels. That canal is short and you can walk the dry
canal's length from the top all the way down to the river through a
deep, primitive-looking cut. At 15 miles, the Great Falls Tavern on
the Maryland side is now a C & O museum and a good spot to take
a break.

16.6: Swain's Lock has a concession stand and canoe/bike rentals. The canal is watered at this point. The first H/B/O is here.
Many DC camping adventurers attempt to overnight at Swain's.

22: Our first aqueduct, the Seneca Aqueduct.

26: Horsepen Branch H/B/O, more than likely our first camping
spot.

35: Whites Ferry. We are in Civil War country now. A concession
stand and various rentals are available here. A beached ferry boat,
the *Jubal Early*, is named for the Confederate general who staged an
unsuccessful last-ditch raid attempting to capture Washington, DC,
in the final days of the war.

42: Monocacy Aqueduct, the canal company's showpiece. At
516 feet long, it is the second-largest man-made feature on the canal
(after the Paw Paw Tunnel). The gracefully arched structure has
been badly damaged by hurricanes in the past and has recently been
completely renovated. Walking our bikes across, high above the
water, is fascinating and a highlight of the trip.

48: Point of Rocks. There's quite a bit of activity going on here
with the canal and rival railroad joining up to pass on the narrow
ledge together. A (now fixed) pivot bridge, lock 28, and an H/B/O
are all here. This is a favorite place for folks who live nearby to walk
and bike. When I biked the canal some years ago, a youngster on a
bicycle approached my friend and me and memorably asked, "Do
you know any good bike trails around here?"

51.5: Catoctin Creek Aqueduct. The busy activity of the capital district is fading as the scenery becomes increasingly rural. There is a whole different feel to this leg of the trip. By bike we are beginning the third day of the ride, and we've seen lots of interesting locks, lock tenders homes, and historic structures. The one constant is the Potomac.

The area around Frederick, MD, has many historic places that are worth exploring after our ride is over. Civil War enthusiasts should not miss Antietam Battlefield in Sharpsburg, site of one of the bloodiest battles of the Civil War. These days the battlefield is quiet, peaceful farmland with monuments and cannon paying tribute to the many fallen soldiers. Washington Monument State Park, east of Hagerstown, features the first monument built to honor the president. It was dedicated in 1827 and looks like a two-story stone milk bottle. The more famous Washington Monument in DC was dedicated in 1885.

57.6: Small factory ruins.

60: Sandy Hook, a good supply stop.

60.6: Bridges and remains of bridges cross the Potomac on the way to Harpers Ferry. This is the beginning of major ruin hunting, and Civil War history comes fast and furious. Our old pal, the Appalachian Trail, joins in for a short time before crossing over to Harpers Ferry. There is a youth hostel near here, on the canal side of the river, which gives us some welcome relief from all the primitive camping we've done, not to mention also giving us the prospect for a real shower.

Harpers Ferry National Historic Park is attractive and a natural place to take a break from all the spine-jarring trail riding. Plan to spend a day here and take advantage of a restaurant. This is also an opportunity to learn about John Brown's famous 1849 raid on the armory along the Potomac River. Interesting mill ruins sit by the Shenandoah River, and Lock 33 along the canal is also a good ruin.

Write to the park for brochures and information: Harpers Ferry National Historic Park, Box 65, Harpers Ferry, WV 25425.

61: The Maryland Heights Trail (roughly 1.75 miles round trip) runs from a trailhead accessed from the towpath and climbs up the bluff opposite Harper's Ferry, eventually ending at Overlook Cliff.

Along the way, the trail passes three gun batteries and stone fort ruins. This is a very difficult, steep trail, and I do not recommend taking a break from the C&O to hike it; save it for another time.

69: Antietam Creek Aqueduct Recreation Area. Three beehive-shaped lime kilns, remnants from the thriving iron-making days, are all that remain of the industrial village once extant for a half mile along the banks of the creek. Here, iron from local deposits was forged into weapons and also the usual farm implements. The ironworks were most active in the 1840s, sometimes shipping pig iron via the canal to Harpers Ferry for additional refinement. Additionally, various different mills at this site (grist, shingle, spinning, and saw) used waterpower to manufacture their goods and the canal to ship them out. The 140-foot aqueduct is a few hundred feet south of the parking area.

69.6: Antietam Creek Ranger Station (National Park Service); phone 301-432-6348.

75.6: Several caves, known as the Sharpsburg Shelter Caves, are in this section.

88: More caves in this area.

This section of the canal is the first one that I explored with my friend Dave (who lived in the area), and I have many good memories

Lock near Hagerstown

of days spent exploring the canal's secrets. We got muddy together crawling into caves and walking through mucked up old locks whenever I drove down from New York City to visit him.

I found out about the C & O in a roundabout way. Dave and I are childhood buddies, and when he moved down to Hagerstown, MD, in the 1980s, we wrote to each other from time to time. In one of my letters, I thought that I still had room in the envelope for my postage stamp's weight allowance, so I stuffed some Chinese food receipts, used napkins, credit card blanks, and other stuff into the envelope. In his next letter, Dave reciprocated with likewise useless junk.

One letter he sent contained a C & O pamphlet from the National Park Service, plus other C & O literature. Not all the paper we packed into the envelopes was useless. Good things were hidden between the business cards, sales brochures, and magazine tear cards. The C & O material intrigued me because I liked ruins and ghost towns even back then, so on my next visit, we got the Towpath Guide out of a library and went to work exploring. In 1987, we biked it together end to end. Mostly.

Towpath near Williamsport

92.11: Dellingers Cave.

92.25: We're halfway. Three to four days from Washington by bike at an average of 25–30 miles per day.

99: Williamsport, the canal town that was the nation's capital for twenty-eight hours during the Revolution. Steel-framed Western Maryland Railroad bridges make worthy photographic subjects in the late afternoon's golden light.

106 to 109: Plenty of lift locks and related structures relating to the Dam #5 complex are here to explore. Check out the ruin of the mule crossover bridge at mile 107. Four Locks at mile 109 are particularly noteworthy. We're starting to gain in elevation more seriously now.

112: Fort Frederick State Park is a restored 1756 stone fort that features summer reenactments. The park is a worthwhile place to explore while taking a break from the bumpy, muddy towpath.

116: Licking Creek Aqueduct. Ruins of the old aqueduct are near a hiker/biker/overnighter campsite. Make camp here if it is a reasonable place to break, and then we can examine the aqueduct and walk down to the river. Interstate noise can at times be intrusive, however, which is the only drawback to this spot.

123: Tonoloway Creek Aqueduct and an adjoining lift lock.

123.5: Town of Hancock, MD. After following a generally northwestern heading from our start at the nation's capital, the canal and Potomac now bend more toward the west. This is a good supply point, and there are restaurants and motels in town if we need a change of pace for a night or two. The National Park Service runs a small C & O Canal Visitor Center and museum that we need to see at 326 East Main Street; phone 301-678-5463.

127.4: Round Top Cement Mill. This is a major point of interest on our adventure. Dating from 1837, it's the most accessible old ruin on the towpath. Interpretive signs posted along the canal tell the history of the place.

H/B/O campsites are getting more and more remote. Trains chugging through on the other side of the river are the most frequent reminder that we aren't totally removed from civilization.

154.5: A dramatic series of lift locks that are the precursor to the spectacular Paw Paw Tunnel. Once we start exploring these locks,

Round Top Cement Mill

Inside Paw Paw Tunnel

we know the tunnel is just ahead, and we've been looking forward to going through it from our first day on the path!

155: Paw Paw Tunnel. This is it, the major feature and heavy hitter of the trip. At 3,118 feet long, the tunnel cuts through the hard mountain rock to avoid a 6-mile series of bends in the Potomac.

We may want to pass through it a few times, just to take it all in. Bring a flashlight to examine the bricks lining the walls, and look for tow-rope burns on the rail. An interesting effect is the way the dot of light from the portal at the opposite end of the tunnel appears to maintain its size until we are very close to exiting. Fellow tunnel explorers' dark silhouettes against the portal openings form ghostly shapes as we walk through. Indistinct voices seem to whisper at us through the damp air near the eastern end of the tunnel.

The last 30 miles pass peacefully through the Maryland countryside toward the western terminus, where there is an excellent bike shop and Park Service visitor center.

184.5: Cumberland, MD: the "Queen City of the Alleghenies." End of the trail. Turn around and go back to DC.

5
CAMP HERO

For a certain segment of the population, 415-acre Camp Hero may very well be the Holy Grail of Road to Ruins exploration. Some of us got very excited when we found out it had finally been opened to the public (although it has been a state park for twenty years) for proper visitation. Sneaking in is *so* 1980s.

The Camp Hero/Montauk Point area has been inhabited since the days of the Montauk tribe. The lighthouse at the point was constructed (under authority of George Washington) in 1795, and Teddy Roosevelt's Rough Riders assembled in the area for R&R sometime around 1900, following the Spanish-American War.

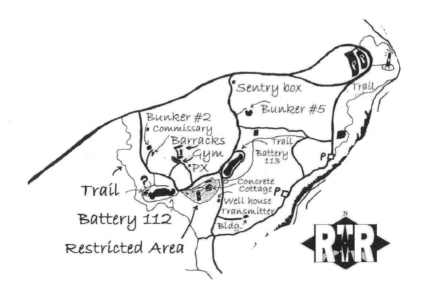

Coastal defenses went up in 1942. The base was named for U.S. Army Major General Andrew Hero Jr., the chief of coastal artillery between the world wars.

An odd feature of the base, circa 1942, was that it was designed to appear as a small coastal village to enemy air reconnaissance. About 650 enlisted men lived amid what appeared to be peaceful Cape Cod–style homes and even a church with a steeple (actually a gymnasium). In 1947, the base was placed on inactive status and then demilitarized in 1949.

The renamed Montauk Air Force Station defended the New York area with its new sophisticated radar (the Semi-Automated Ground Environment, or SAGE system) from 1951 to 1957. The radar tower arrived in 1960 and is 120 feet wide, 40 feet high, and weighs in at about 80,000 pounds.

From 1981, when the site was deactivated for the last time, until the present day, is when things got interesting. Let me tell you the strange but true story of how I first got involved with Camp Hero.

In the spring of 1987, my friend Marcus belonged to a camera club in Brooklyn. At the same time I was studying photography at a local college, so we would go out shooting every weekend. Even back then I was attracted to ghost towns and similar abandoned locations, so we would poke around places like defunct Roosevelt Raceway on Long Island, old forts, and the like. We eventually become fairly organized and did a few notably successful investigative missions in later years as the IMF Photo Team, a rotating group of urban explorers.

One night I went to a photo club meeting with Marcus. After the meeting, we went out to dinner with one of Marcus's friends from the club. I'll call him Jon. Jon was a tall, gangly guy with arthritic hands. He had been printing some shots in the club's darkroom that night and at dinner Marcus asked me, "Did you see Jon's picture?"

"No" I said, not knowing what picture he was referring to.

Jon showed me a print. I didn't think much of it, but a few days later I had to see it again.

A week later, Marcus and I went over to Jon's apartment in Brooklyn to get a better look. He met us at the door and escorted us in. Eight-by-ten-inch black-and-white prints were piled up from floor to ceiling in the small place. Jon pulled out a handful of prints from one stack, and we went over to the kitchen table where the light was better. I got my second look.

The image was a cropped blowup from a larger frame. It showed an antiaircraft gun emplacement (Battery 112) of World War II vintage. These batteries are sometimes referred to as "bunkers," but that terminology is technically incorrect. It looks like a big wall of concrete with an opening that's about 20 feet above ground level, where the gun used to be. There is a semicircular brim a few feet above the opening, where a curtain used to hang, which could be drawn around the gun to hide it from enemy aircraft. The roof is covered with earth: in fact, most of the structure is camouflaged that way. So we have this emplacement, probably 40 or so feet high. Outside of the emplacement, on the left side of the picture and behind the main structure, was a figure in dark silhouette. It was about two-thirds the size of the emplacement (putting it at about 25 feet high) and vaguely apelike in appearance. It assumed a hunched over posture, its right hand and arm appearing to be in front of the creature while the emplacement obscured the rest of the body. The top half of a rounded head protruded up from the wide, curved shoulders.

Battery 112 today

Jon had several prints (most in black and white, but some from color slides) with differently filtered exposures, contrasts, and blow-ups of this creature (which he called "Junior"), trying to pull some detail out of the dark shape. Junior was not giving up any secrets that way.

"What is it?" I asked him.

Jon told me that out by Montauk Point stood the remains of the old Air Force base called Camp Hero. It is state-owned property, but at the time closed to the public. He belongs to a group of researchers called the American Psychotronic Association that uses electronics (vacuum tubes in particular are popular with them) to measure psychic phenomena. Their measurements pointed out to Camp Hero, and there, after gaining entry permission from the office of Senator Barry Goldwater, they climbed up inside the radar tower building and took photographs of the area. The psychotronic investigators didn't physically see Junior behind the structure at the time, but they took panoramic photos of the area from the top, and he appeared on some of their prints after they were developed.

Well, this was all very interesting, especially the description he gave of the base. I was thinking it was a place I needed to see. Of course, I had many questions about Junior, also. Jon invited us to the American Psychotronic Association's next meeting, where we could meet with them and get the answers we were looking for.

In the time between the meeting with Jon and when we actually met the A.P.A., Marcus and I did some homework and called the military historian at Fort Hamilton in Brooklyn. He had never even heard of Camp Hero. He did tell me that similar installations were on the Rockaway Peninsula (Fort Tilden) and at Sandy Hook in New Jersey. These places were formal parks and open to the public.

BEGIN PHASE 1: PREPARATION

Over the next few weekends we visited both places, familiarizing ourselves with the gun casemates, or "batteries." In those days (the late 1980s), Fort Tilden's batteries were closed and gated off but easy to sneak into, which we did more than once. Some go down a few stories into the damp pitch darkness. Tilden also has some building shells on the surface and the remains of a Nike missile installation. It was a good place to warm up.

Some strange coincidences added icing to this unusual cake as we prepared our mission profile. I was visiting a friend of mine one day as his sisters were watching a sitcom on television concerning high school students at their science fair. As I passed through the room, one character mentioned the name of his project: "psycho-tronics." True, he used it to read his girlfriend's mind, but it isn't a word one hears every day. How strange I should be passing by at that exact moment. A newspaper ran a Sunday pictorial of abandoned New York City area military sites, including an aerial photograph of Camp Hero. Another time, when I was listening to the radio one night, searching around the dial for those low-powered stations you only hear in the early hours, I came across a discussion of the evil doings at the base. Think about it: a station I've never heard before, at a time I rarely listen, discussing Camp Hero, and I happened to stumble across the conversation. When I last went out to Camp Hero to research this book, a local newspaper was running a story on the base. Another coincidence?

PHASE 2: THE MEETING

Finally the day came when we were due to meet with the American Psychotronic Association. The plan was that we would come in after their meeting (which was closed to non-members because of the high security risk) and at that time ask them what we wanted to know about Junior. Marcus and I drove over to a high-rise apartment building on the west side of Manhattan. Walking to the building after we parked the car, I said to him, "This is going to be weird. We have to play it straight, and be careful not to laugh or insult them."

We took the elevator up and knocked on the door. A serious-looking heavyset fellow with jet-black slicked down hair and dark sunglasses opened it and let us in. The group was in the living room, while three others were in a small kitchen area just beyond. The ringleader, Coynes (all names are pseudonyms), was the guy who opened the door. He planted himself on a couch and stayed put for the rest of the time we were there, sitting solo, the cushions around him pushed up in protest. His shirt was a size too small and the buttons strained to stay closed. He didn't smile once.

Another fellow, Carr, didn't seem to be unusual in any way; indeed, he seemed to be the "normal" person in that crowd. Years later, some members of this group or a similar one became involved with federal law enforcement after attempting to poison local politicians on Long Island (because they prevented access to places like Camp Hero) by slipping them radium-laced toothpaste. I believe that Carr was among that group.

There was another man there whose name I never knew. I remember thinking that if Charlie Brown was a real person, he'd look like this guy. Jon was also there, blending in perfectly.

That was the crew in the living room. In the kitchenette sat a pair of older women who looked alike and never said a word, accompanied by a wizened old man who was also quiet during the interview.

Marcus and I introduced ourselves and thanked them for their time. We told them that based on Jon's picture, our intention was to go out to Camp Hero twice: our upcoming recon objective that Saturday was to get the lay of the land, check out the base, and attempt to get a picture of Junior. Our primary mission was a few weeks later and was intended to be a more thorough penetration of the structures and an attempt to corroborate what Jon had told us.

With Coynes moderating, I starting asking questions. He seemed to be irritated and answered in short sentences, often answering questions with questions. As we began the interview, Charlie Brown pulled out a tape recorder.

"Can I tape this?" he asked.

"No!" Coynes said sharply. "Take the tape out. Show it to me." Unhappily, Charlie did as he was commanded. I was taking notes with a pen and pad, which the big man didn't seem to mind.

"What is Junior?" I asked.

He is an extradimensional being. After the military left the camp, a few years passed before another group came on the scene. Secret in nature and part of a shadow U.S. government, they were involved in mind-control experimentation using huge amounts of power. A psychic was strapped down into the "famous" Montauk Chair and huge amounts of power, generated in a building on-site, was channeled through him, sent up the antenna on the radar building, and then broadcast out over the eastern end of Long Island.

In a nearby restaurant, one moment everything was fine and calm, but then the malevolent psychic broadcast began and bedlam ensued. Fights broke out, damage was done, and people were killing each other. The experiment abruptly ended; amid the calm but bloody aftermath no one could recall what just happened. These experiments took place in the 1970s as this secret group built a research complex five stories under the ground in an attempt to remain undiscovered.

The nefarious schedule continued until the day something went terribly wrong. During a particularly powerful experiment, the unforeseen occurred. As a huge current swelled around the "Chair," a door between dimensions opened, and the monstrous Junior stepped out. He went on a furious rampage, killing everyone he could get his paws on until someone managed to cut the power (with an axe to the power grid). The door closed shut on Junior, and there he is to this day, stuck behind the casemate, 20 feet tall, frozen between dimensions, waiting for his chance to continue his mindless assault.

"Did you go back after getting the picture?" I asked Coynes.

"No, why should we? We got the proof that we wanted."

Marcus asked him, "Is it safe to go out there?"

"Unmarked police cars patrol the area. Whoever those cops are, they'll arrest anyone they catch trespassing on the base."

During further conversation, it was revealed that there was an underground submarine base on the site, also. They couldn't tell us where it was or how we could get into it. They told us about the radar building and the spot behind the gun batteries where Junior was stuck. They told us that radio tubes act as "psychic valves" and were useful for measuring paranormal activity.

We continued with the questions, but their answers were vague and unsatisfying. As we were getting ready to leave, the old man at the kitchen table spoke up: "Would you like to consult the Pendulum?" We walked over to him. He produced a sphere of wax that was about the size of a golf ball; a single strand of thick copper wire spiraled around it from top to bottom. He suspended the pendulum from his hand by a thin, clear filament that looked like fishing line. Yes, we wanted to: maybe we'd get solid answers from it. The old man started rotating the Pendulum in slow circles an inch or so above the kitchen table as the group looked on and then, as he concentrated on it, he said we could start asking it questions.

"Is Junior out there at Camp Hero?"

"Yes," the old man said, as he stared at his circling wax ball.

"Will we get a picture of him?" Yes.

"Will we get arrested next week when we go out there?" No.

"Will we get into the radar building?" Yes.

We couldn't think of anything else. Then the old man asked us, "Would you like me to put a Dome of White Light around you?" We didn't want to be rude, but we had to know a little more about that! "What does it do?" Marcus asked. "It will protect the both of you from harm when you go out there."

We looked at each other and said, "Yes." That was it.

We left the meeting, not believing a word of this but still fascinated with the whole situation. We wondered whether Jon was going to be executed for his serious security lapse.

PHASE 3: THE RECON

It's nearly a three-hour drive out to Montauk Point from Queens. You don't see any sign of the air force base until you're almost at the Point. At one particular high spot on Montauk Highway the radar building and that huge dish on the roof suddenly appear off in the distance as the drive east pushes on. Then the road dips and it's gone forever.

Once we knew that the side roads we passed went into the camp, we drove slowly past the base gates along Montauk Highway. After a quick recon of the entrances, we parked by the lighthouse and got our gear together. Although the signs said clearly to keep out, the fences were bent and full of holes and gaps. Those shadow-government boys didn't keep up the housework, it seemed. Once in, we started out toward the radar building and took pictures as we went along. The place was very quiet. We heard the Atlantic Ocean crashing on the beach a few hundred yards away and the wind blowing through the trees. Sounds of cars driving on the nearby road made it seem as if those malevolent "Men in Black" policemen would suddenly appear at any moment and hustle us off to some holding cell

Inspecting the grounds

six stories down. We walked in silence, ready to bolt into the brush at a second's notice, but we never needed to.

It was hard resisting going into the many open buildings we passed, but we had to keep our objective in mind. Infiltration of any structures would have to wait. Approaching the radar building, our excitement grew. There was an open door at the base of the building! We walked up and went inside, but not very far. We looked into the open first floor and then came out again. Stay focused. The building is on the highest point of land at the base and affords a good view of the surrounding area, and the gun emplacements were in clear sight. There are actually two of them a few hundred feet apart. We both took pictures and looked over at them through binoculars, but we sure didn't see any extradimensional apelike monsters hiding anywhere near them. We exited the base through another nearby gate and walked back to the car along Montauk Highway. On the way back, we checked out some old submarine lookout towers west of the base, at Shadmoor State Park. So far, our mission was a success.

A week or so later, when I got the pictures back, I almost jumped out of my skin. I did it! I had a picture of Junior! He was standing in a hunched-over, opaque silhouette next to the concrete bunker, just like in Jon's picture. Marcus was with his family in Ocean City, MD, so I called him there immediately.

"Marcus! Guess who I have a picture of!"

"Me?" he said. I would have slapped him if he were next to me.

"No, not *you,* I have a picture of Junior!" We both whooped like kids. It was great. Man, were we ever raring to go back. As an aside, I showed the picture of the encasements and the shadow behind it to a Latin coworker of mine. He looked at it and said "Yeti" without missing a beat.

Then it hit me: the Pendulum was right. We found Junior, didn't get busted by Men in Black, and gained entry to the radar building. How long was that Dome good for? We were going back soon.

PHASE 4: THE MISSION

A few weeks later, our team was completed as "G.I." Joe joined Marcus and me as we set off to explore Camp Hero properly. Joe was a tough-talking member of the same camera club Marcus belonged to and had seen Jon's picture also. Marcus had previously called Carr from the psychotronic group and invited him along. Carr's response was now that the government knew about our plans and it was dangerous to continue. "How do they know?" Marcus asked. Carr told him his phone was bugged. That was that. Carr didn't go with us.

Upon reaching the Montauk parking lot, we set out for the closest gate into the camp. Our objectives for this infiltration were:

1. Access the camp
2. Enter the radar building
3. Explore the other buildings
4. Try to verify the psychotronic story as much as possible
5. Check out the emplacements
6. Look for the sub base
7. Look for the secret underground lab complex
8. Look for Junior
9. Don't get caught
10. Take plenty of pictures

Entering the grounds was easy. On highest alert mode and ready for anything, the nascent IMF Photo Team walked silently in single file up the road and toward the main group of buildings. The

Radar building

Open doors in the radar building

close surf and wind through the trees still sounded like approaching cars. After a while we got used to it, feeling a bit more relaxed but still cautious. We entered several of the buildings, taking care not to damage anything. We all took many pictures, savoring the buildup to the first big event: entering the radar building.

The building itself is massive and gray. Standing at the base of the building and looking up, the first thing you notice is that huge ovular antenna sticking out at the top that doesn't rotate any longer but twists ever so slightly. Our side door was still open, so we readied our flashlights and helped ourselves inside. The three of us walked into the open space on the ground floor. The floor was wet. It was dark. Machinery was everywhere. As we were about to start climbing the steps to the next floor, Marcus found a breaker panel and to my amazement turned on the lights. How odd that after all these years there is still power to the building. Who pays the electric bill? Conspiracy theories are beginning to come into focus.

We started our ascent up the tower. We would enter each floor and then each go our separate ways, taking pictures and exploring in silence. Every floor had something different: dead panels of electronics, papers strewn around, and instruments long quiet all these years. Even with the lights on it was dark, since there were no windows on the lower levels. Finally, after thoroughly exploring the floors on the way up, we made our way to the topmost level. It was actually the height of two stories with a catwalk halfway up, surrounding the antenna base and controls. That huge antenna was right above us. We walked around the space and did our individual explorations, and then as if on cue the three of us all came together at the same time in the center of the floor. The light of one opening illuminated the scene.

"This is too easy," Marcus said with a slightly amused look on his face.

At that exact moment, a long low groan, seemingly lasting forever, drifted through the room from one side to the other. The sound was like an old man moaning in pain, wavering only a little. It probably only lasted for a few seconds but we all looked at each other during the duration of the groan with a new concern. Suddenly, this became more than a game.

"Okay, that was weird," I said a few moments after it stopped. Silence. We were still looking at each other.

"The antenna, twisting in the wind," Joe figured aloud. Most likely he was right. It made sense.

We regrouped mentally and continued our investigation. Passing signs warning of a "Radiation Hazard," we climbed the last set of steel ladders that brought us out and onto the roof of the radar building. What a spectacular view! The Atlantic Ocean, the lighthouse, the other buildings, and of course Battery 112 (Junior's new home) were all laid out in a bright panorama below us on that sunny day. We did a binocular survey of the battery with no apparent sign of our extradimensional friend. I took a few pictures of the scene with my telephoto lens and then it was time to begin our final investigation: Junior and his encasements.

Marcus shut the lights off as we exited the building. Walking downhill, we found other buildings to check out. One had huge generators, some of which were wrapped in paper. This was obviously the powerhouse, and it was a spooky experience. Tools were left lying around. A fire extinguisher was sitting on a desk as if it was about to be put to use at any moment. A paintbrush was sitting in a can of thinner, the dust of years sitting thick upon it. This building definitely had the feeling of quick abandonment throughout, but try as we might, we didn't see any evidence of power being physically cut. (Did we interpret the A.P.A.'s story too literally?) Those big generators must have been able to crank out some impressive wattage, however. If you needed big juice, this certainly was the place to get it.

After more exploration of other smaller structures, we found ourselves outside the first battery. It was most impressive up close; however, that huge open doorway in the high face of cold, mottled concrete didn't look very inviting. Walking up to the entrance, we discovered that it led straight through to another opening on the other side. We went in and saw that a few feet inside and to our left was a long, dark hallway with a dot of light at the other end: the second gun position. Three flashlights quickly came out of our backpacks, flash units went on top of the cameras and we started to slowly walk down the cool, musty corridor toward Junior.

Out footsteps echoed through the square hallway as we made the journey in silence. Flashlight beams cut the darkness, sliding down walls and up ceilings, across rails and into side rooms. Corridors appeared every so often, some leading to rooms that we ventured into, others leading to rooms accessed by slits that were too narrow for any of us to easily fit through. Not even the fearless G.I. Joe dared to try. If one had to quickly exit that pitch-black space behind the slit, there would be no way to possibly do it. All the rooms we checked out were completely empty and silent, as if cleared of any damning artifacts of evil experimentation.

The dot of light from the far opening widened and intensified as we neared the exit. Finishing the corridor walk, standing at the portal of the second gun emplacement, we were very aware that the focus of our quest was standing in frozen stasis right around the corner. We put fresh rolls of film into our cameras and new batteries into the flashes, as if we were loading our weapons. Again, we exchanged glances. This is what it's all about!

I ordered Marcus to go out there. He told Joe to go. Joe asked me why I didn't want to go first. We laughed and walked out together. Turning the corner, there we were, standing right in front of an extradimensional monster caught in a time/space warp. Except, we didn't see anything. We all took pictures. There was a small fire hydrant close to the ground and an evergreen in back of it. It was a darker green than the surrounding vegetation. Junior was a tree.

We walked back to the car through the base. At that point we didn't really care if Men in Black bothered us. Mission accomplished. Shedding our backpacks at the car, Marcus and I went to the snack bar at the lighthouse for a bite. I was first back to the car. Marcus came running out soon afterward.

"Paul Simon is in there," he said. Marcus is a *major* Paul Simon fan.

"Get his autograph," I said.

"I don't have a pen." I gave him a pen.

"I don't have paper." I gave him the wrapper of the candy bar I just bought.

He went back in but Paul and his lady friend had left and were heading out to the beach. Marcus didn't follow; the moment had passed.

I told this story to some coworkers in Seattle recently. When one of them, Kate, came to New York, she wanted to see Camp Hero. Fourteen years after our first mission, Marcus and I returned with Kate to the camp. (None of us have seen Joe since then.) "Closed" and "No Trespassing" signs were still there on the fences, as were the well-worn paths around them. The radar building entrance was sealed. Battery 112 was sealed. Holes had been pecked into the reinforced concrete as if some paranoid holdouts were still trying to find the shadow government installation or the sub base. There was no sign of Junior, either, just like there wasn't all those years earlier.

On September 18, 2002, the New York State Office of Parks, Recreation and Historic Preservation officially opened Camp Hero to the public, although it has been a state park since 1984. Maps are available at kiosks that are scattered about the base. With the park map in hand, we can finally spend the day wandering around and inspecting the structures while marveling all the time at that huge radar building with the last intact AN/FPS-35 radar dish still in existence. The Men in Black have been evicted, it seems.

There is a parking area on Col. Daniel Wolf Road just north of the radar tower group that is a good central base of operations. Following the map we picked up at the kiosk, let's head north to the group of buildings noted as an exchange store, gymnasium, and bowling alley. All we can do is look, since all of the structures are sealed tightly and none are accessible.

After poking around the area, we'll follow Col. Daniel Wolf Road (in front of us) downhill to the next right turn, Camp Hero Road. We'll walk down to a point at which the commissary building is up a hill to our right, and then head up there and look around. The map indicates Bunker 2 is around here someplace. From what we already know about military camouflage techniques vis-à-vis "bunkers" (from all the crawling around we've done following the hikes in this book), we correctly guess that the bunker is below us and slightly to the north. When we go down there, we see it's another small, sealed concrete structure. No access.

Following the fence around will bring us back onto Camp Hero Road near a sentry booth. The road goes uphill toward the tower, but we should veer off onto a red-blazed trail that circles Battery 112, passing our extradimensional friend on the far end as we circle the structure and come back to the road. Continuing uphill, when we get to the parking area for the radar tower group, we see the entire facility has been fenced off, preventing access.

Oh, the irony! In opening the park to the public, the New York State Office of Parks, Recreation and Historic Preservation made the most interesting parts of the ground inaccessible. When the place was "closed," we had free access to all the buildings and structures, and now that it's open, we can't enter any of them. And while I'm at it, is it only coincidence that the only clear views of Junior (from the top of the radar tower and the hill's high point by the entrance to the tower) are now sealed off? Is it the shadow governmental circles within circles at work, still securing the scene of the crime after all those years? Someday, the radar building may be reopened as a museum. If so, you might see us there for the fourth time or even a fifth.

From the parking area and kiosk near the radar tower, heading south on Col. John Dunn Road will bring us by a well house and transmitter building before running into Old Montauk Highway. Bearing left (east), we'll take that trail past the fishing permit parking lot, eventually reaching Battery 216. Bearing left (northwest) on Coast Artillery Road, we'll make a quick left and then right at the first intersection we come to (Rough Riders Road) and pick up the Battery 113 trail. None of the hiking trails today, or even in the area, offer any kind of impressive viewpoints until they reach the ocean.

Back at the tower lot, we can bear right, heading straight down Camp Hero Road (which goes straight at the next intersection, past a sawhorse saying the area is closed to vehicular traffic) and investigate the old ball field and our last bunker, #5.

Turning around, we'll follow Camp Hero Road back to our car. Restrooms and picnic tables make the spot a good place for a lunch break, where we might plot future Island operations:

- Shadmoor State Park, 4 miles west off Route 27, is a small park with dramatically eroded 50-foot bluffs overlooking the Atlantic Ocean. Great photographic opportunities are here, particularly early and late in the day when the sun cuts across the dunes at sharp angles. On site are two left-over spotting towers related to Camp Hero. They are both sealed and not enterable.
- The "Places That Aren't Mentioned" appendix discusses Muttontown Preserve, a mansion ruin in Syosset.

Junior

6
THE CORNISH ESTATE

WHERE: North of Cold Spring, NY
WHY: Estate and dairy farm ruin and reservoir, plus an insane hike up Breakneck Ridge
DIFFICULTY: Moderate; 5 miles once you get up Breakneck
MAP: New York–New Jersey Trail Conference Map: East Hudson Trails
DIRECTIONS: Taconic State Parkway to Route 301 west. Take Route 301 west toward Cold Spring. Make a right turn (north) on Route 9D, and go 2.2 miles to some parking areas on the left, just past the tunnel

While it is true you can hike straight to the Cornish estate and dairy farm ruins along the Brook Trail (red-blazed), it is far more rewarding to hike up mighty Breakneck Ridge and return past the estate on the way back. There is a sense of accomplishment in doing this that is difficult to accurately describe.

That's our plan. Keep in mind that we have to get here early, since this is one of the most popular hiking trails in the area and parking fills up quickly. Don't forget to grab your flashlight. Let's tackle Breakneck!

The Breakneck Ridge Trail (white-blazed) starts on the western side of Route 9D, just north of the highway tunnel. This trail starts out steep and then goes straight up, passing by some sheer cliffs and dangerous turns, so I definitely recommend doing this particular hike in good weather. Frequent scrambling, or using hands and feet to climb up, is required on this trail. The peak is

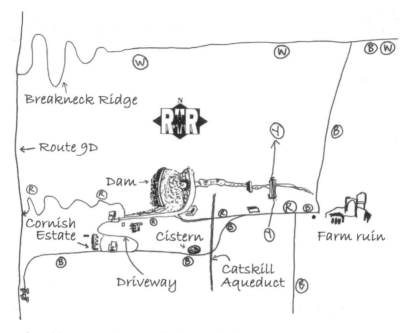

only a bit over a linear mile from the beginning, but the rise tops out at about 1,200 feet. Insidiously, there are four false summits with tremendous views before you reach the true summit, which really has no view.

At the highest false summit, look around. To your south, on the other side of the Hudson River sits the United States Military Academy at West Point. On the right, we can't miss abandoned, exploded Bannerman's Castle on Pollopel Island. Straight ahead is Storm King Mountain. Mount Taurus is to the left (south) on the other side of the valley. It is higher, at about 1,400 feet, but this trail is far steeper. Far below us is Route 9D.

At 1.5 miles from the start (it seems like 10) the blue-blazed Notch Trail crosses. To extend the hike at some future date, continue on past this point to a woods road 1.25 miles away. Follow that to the left, where it will connect with the Wilkinson Memorial Trail (yellow-blazed). We learned about Mr. Wilkinson in the Beacon Mountain Casino chapter. Anyway, the purpose of this extension of the hike is to lead us up over Sugarloaf North, where we will get the best possible look at Bannerman's Castle on Pollopel Island. Francis

Bannerman was a munitions dealer who built his massive home on top of broken rock from New York City subway excavations. An explosion in the 1920s blew a wall out, but it was repaired and business went on as usual. Eventually the island was acquired by the New York State Parks and Recreation Department, which removed most of the weapons and gunpowder. Not all of the dangerous stuff was removed, however: vandals in 1969 set a fire that touched off a massive explosion, blowing some parts of the castle across the river and onto the train tracks.

For now, let's stick to the original plan. We'll take the Notch Trail to the right (east) and follow it down to where it connects with a woods road, but stays blue. Soon enough we see the pond, dam, and remains of the Cornish estate dairy farm. Get that flashlight ready! A massive stone barn ruin and plenty of other ruined buildings keep us contentedly exploring (and guessing usage) for a while.

The Notch turns left (east), but we will continue straight downhill on the Brook Trail (red-blazed). A concrete pump house is passed on the right. The large cylindrical concrete structure further down was a drinking water cistern, filtering water from Breakneck Brook for the estate just ahead. Explore the side trails that wander around through here, but do not get lost! We have important ruins

Farm site

Inside the barn

to discover and can't waste time looking for you. The wide area we pass through on the way down is the Catskill Aqueduct.

The red trail eventually drops down to meet broken concrete pavement and the Cornish water works. To our right are the remains of another pump house, and beyond that, the brook cascades through a tunnel into the overgrown dammed pond in front of us. As we hike down the red trail, there are two more ruined stone structures on the hill to our left that need our attention.

Further down the trail, the path widens and we see a structure on our right with a fallen roof. The red trail bends sharply right as it leaves the road and heads down through the woods, but we have another agenda right now. Continue straight over a concrete slab "bridge" and encounter the impressive estate, even in ruin, of Mr. Edward G. Cornish.

Cornish was the wealthy chairman of the board of the National Lead Company. His estate dates from the early 1900s. Mr. Cornish died during the 1930s, causing the property to be tied up in litigation. It was sealed during that time, but a fire in 1956 began the process of destruction that we see today. In recent years volunteers have cleared away the brambles and overgrowth, easing exploration of the site.

The mansion

Approach the main entrance from the circular driveway. Peek over the vanished floor into the living room and check out the archways, double fireplaces, and fancy diamond tiles. It must have been quite the place back in the day. We can find the family's mountain-reflective swimming pool on the other, river-facing side of the estate.

If we had continued straight past the house (instead of bearing left), we'd see a blue trail appear. Roughly a quarter-mile uphill to the left is a large, circular, rock-lined, tanklike structure about 20 feet in diameter. But we didn't go straight.

Continue on the driveway, passing a once formal garden on the left, and be prepared to be impressed by the huge multileveled greenhouse. With flashlight in hand, we can do a fast inspection of the basement.

The driveway then bends to the right and drops through the woods to Route 9D. We will work our way around (to the left) back to the red Brook Trail and continue down that way.

The Brook Trail brings us to the road, and our car is to the right (north) about a half-mile up. The best part of the walk back is passing by the incomparable Breakneck Ridge and looking up the awesome rock face trying to see the top, while thinking "Did I just hike *that*?"

Fireplace

The pool

7
CRANBERRY LAKE PRESERVE

Cranberry Lake Preserve is a small (165-acre), intimate county preserve that protects wetlands near the Kensico Reservoir. Farm site and powder storage shed foundations await our attention within, and there is also an old quarry with some interesting artifacts to seek out.

The nature center hours are currently 9 A.M. to 4 P.M., Tuesday through Sunday (seasonal hours), but one can park outside the

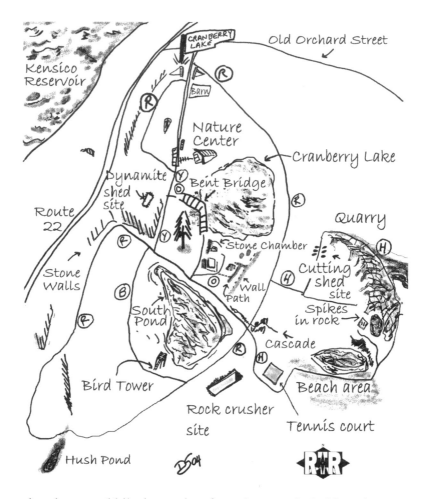

Old Orchard Street

Kensico Reservoir

CRANBERRY LAKE

Barn

Nature Center

Cranberry Lake

Dynamite shed site

Bent Bridge

Quarry

Route 22

Stone Chamber

Cutting shed site

Stone Walls

Wall Path

Spikes in rock

South Pond

Cascade

Bird Tower

Rock crusher site

Beach area

Tennis court

Hush Pond

closed gate and hike in anytime from dawn to dusk. If we time our visit correctly, we can see the center first and then smartly explore the preserve.

We'll begin by hiking on the red "Long Way" trail (just before the gate on the left) and make our way in a southerly direction toward the nature center. All of the side trails we encounter at the beginning of our trek (that branch off of the red trail to the right) will head toward the center, so we don't have to be concerned about finding it. Another point of information that we should be aware of is that the green blazes are not really a trail: they radiate out from the nature center to any point in the park. (The green blazes are not on both sides of trees as other colored blazes are.) Thus, to return (or if someone else gets lost or disoriented), just follow the green blazes back to civilization.

Arriving at the nature center, we can stock up on maps and other reading material and then start our adventure. A free black-and-white park map available inside, but be a sport and buy the excellent large, color orienteering map for two dollars. It's much clearer and will help you navigate around the trickier sites. It's worth mentioning that food is not allowed on the trails.

Beginning our stroll down the major gravel road that passes the nature center (yellow-blazed), we will then bear easterly (left) on any trail we like as we head toward the lake. Once there, we'll find the blue Littoral Trail (LIT-tər-əl: *adj.:* of, on, or along the shore). Turn left (north) and follow the trail in a clockwise direction as it circles the lake.

It can get muddy as the trail skirts the lake, sometimes on boardwalks, and monster mutant earthworms inhabit the loose soil under some of them. In summer the bugs make their presence known as they greedily seek out a free hot lunch. Spring and fall are more tolerable. Blue continues to hug the shoreline until the red "Long Way" trail (heading southwesterly) again reappears. Let's hop over to red and begin a gradual climb, watching the high ridge on our left as the trail and the ridge eventually level out together. As the climb begins, through the woods we can spot a rectangular concrete support high on a hill to our left. At a point where the red trail summits at an overlook, a wide path will appear on the left. Let's note our location as we head off into the quarry area.

The quarry supplied granite to the builders of the nearby Kensico Dam. Construction began in 1913 and ended three years ahead of schedule in 1917. After being dynamited free, the stone blocks were carried by a short rail line to an immense crusher capable of processing as much as 250 tons of stone per hour. The processed stone was carried to the construction site a mile away by railroad, now long gone but easily traced. Guess what we're doing later? The crusher and most buildings were removed by the contractor after the dam was completed, per agreement with the county. Some structures survived, such as stone cutting and dynamite storage sheds, until they were removed in later years.

By now you've doubtless noticed the purple "History Trail" blazes on the trees, which pass by most of the historic sites in the preserve. Bearing eastward into the quarry, we'll head straight toward the cliff face. A visible path goes directly to the chopped-up granite hill that supplied the stone. Very *Planet of the Apes*–looking. After snooping around on blazed or unnamed paths that snake around the base of the wall, let's turn around and go back to purple.

Turning to the right (northerly), we'll follow the purple History Trail blazes on a straight path past some stone blocks in a swampy area. We can soon see to our left the top of the support we spotted earlier and five shorter supports alongside it. This was the site of the stone cutting shed and the rail that brought blocks there from the crusher. Lots of cut stone blocks lie about, some appearing to be foundations or supports.

The purple blazes continue around the quarry and lead us to the top but soon peter out, leaving us on our own. By shading to the

right, we'll get the first high views of the hike today, at 465 feet. Various bent rods and beams are embedded in the stone, formerly anchoring the heavy equipment that quarried and moved the liberated stone slabs. As we pick our way along the top, the blazes will reappear and lead us down the left-hand side of the quarry wall onto the floor of the former operation, passing by an axle and wheel assembly from

Spikes in granite

Quarry pond

a quarry rail car. Before we descend, though, see that cubic rock (to the left of a bush) perched near the edge of the shelf, down there by the pond? There are two bent metal hooks to the right of it. We're going to head over there right now.

Once we climb down, circling to the right around the cliff face on a sandy path next to another quarry pond then across a field of broken granite blocks will get us within sight of the rock. If we pick our way along the pond's shoreline, we'll find our way over there. Standing at that rock we'll find three steel wedges (18 T 0604656, 4547579) are still embedded in the granite just a few feet behind it, having never completed the splitting of the rock.

There is one more mystery we need to investigate before we're done with the quarry. Retracing our steps, we'll circle the quarry pond clockwise, passing a sandy area as we go. Bearing westerly on the path of least resistance brings us to a bona fide oddity, a tennis court (18 T 0604575, 4547506) in the middle of nowhere! As we walk around photographing the decaying vine-wrapped fences and interior, I'll mention that the North Quarry Swim Club operated here until 1997, using the old quarry-mined ponds for recreational purposes. There once was a diving board at the deep end of the pond. Some changing buildings were removed when the club closed, but its tennis court remained.

Although the purple blazes head off to the left (southwesterly), then turn right at a ravine and wind up downhill at the cataract, they are occasionally easy to lose, and if you aren't familiar with the preserve, things can get dicey. Therefore, let's continue straight past the tennis court (still heading west, with a slant to the right) and look for the old railroad bed, paralleling a low rock face. Following it to the right (northeast) will bring us back to the purple History Trail, which we can take (to the left, or westerly) back to the red "Long Way" path.

Once we make our way back around to the "Long Way," let's continue southwesterly (to the left) and shortly arrive at a bench sitting alongside an attractive cataract that flows even in drought conditions. Nice spot for a break.

Continuing on red, we're now following the grade of the rail that brought processed granite from the crusher (now above us to the left) down to the dam. The rail terminus was around here somewhere, at the northwest end of the crusher. Shortly, we leave red and pick up another end of the blue Littoral Trail that bears westward past a wooden observation tower that just begs us to climb up for a quiet view of South Pond.

Staying on the blue Littoral Trail, the low boardwalk carries us just over the South Pond's surface when we resume our walk to the west. South Pond is artificial, created in 1913 as the newly built railroad grades pooled up Cranberry Brook. If we walk quietly over the boardwalk in summer, we will spot all kinds of small wildlife in or near the water: fish, frogs, chipmunks, snakes. Some exit the locality with a splash as they do their best to avoid us.

We soon arrive on the other shore. Surely there must be some sort of ruins on this side of the pond to entertain us? Possibly. Note the small stone-walled enclosure we'll pass on the left. When the blue trail hits the other end of the railroad grade, stop for a moment. Looking to the left (westward), we can see where the railway continued through a cut on its way to the dam, and a barely visible spur branched off northward to meet a dynamite shed (site) that we'll soon visit.

Let us bear east (to the right) at this junction, back onto the wide gravel railroad grade. Take it a few yards down to an orange trail intersection.

A left turn (north) will quickly bring us past the reported 1853 home foundation and root cellar of farmer Thomas Cunningham, but interpretation of this site may not be so simple.

Historical documents pinpoint this site as the Cunningham farm, but there are some secrets we can reveal with proper investigation. To do that we need to walk over to the large open stone chamber (which is, most likely, not a root cellar at all), take a look inside and then walk over to the path and then face left, looking south. We see a path straight ahead bordered by a low stone wall opposite a two-tiered stone landform on our left. Heading straight ahead, southerly, down the narrow lane we can admire the stonework as we move to a point about 50 yards down where the path meets with the orange trail. Turning sharply to the left puts us back on the orange trail, but if we look about 50 feet to the northeast we will see another faint pathway that follows a low stone wall, heading in the direction of the chamber but paralleling the blazed trail. Picking our way along the overgrown path brings us to a rock overhang and squared-off enclosure that looks as if it might have been a small walled garden. Cross over the low wall at the end of the path bearing north with the chamber visible on our left, and at about 30 yards we will find more, much smaller, stone structures right ahead of us. One appears to be a miniature chamber with a fallen roof while another miniature

Stone chamber area

Inside of the chamber

(unfinished?) roofless chamber is just ahead on the right, almost directly opposite the large chamber and near a wall that follows the edge of the lake.

We will look at such structures in more detail in the "Stone Chambers of Mead Farm" chapter, where we'll encounter three more of these mysterious structures, but there's some more discussion to be had regarding this site.

There are two types of stone walls here at Cranberry Lake: the older, low, sharp-tipped piled rock walls and the later, more massive and finished-looking, flat-topped boundary walls that were constructed in the late 1910s after the dam was built and quarrying stopped.

Much of the preserve is on land settled as early as the 1800s. Over the years, old farms centered on the lake were combined to form large estates. William R. Smith bought up some sizable property in Cranberry Lake with the intent of reselling it in smaller parcels, but the Great Depression ruined those plans and forced him into foreclosure. The Strauss family eventually acquired the land and sold most of it to Westchester County in 1967.

A hermit known locally as "Jimmy-under-the-rocks" existed in this area sometime in the nineteenth century. Jimmy Johnson, his birth name, formed a crude home made of locally found rock in an area that is now just outside of the southern end of the preserve and laboriously proceeded to build some quizzical structures over the years. There are stone walls that follow nothing, cornering at hillsides for reasons that only he knew, and pens for animals (one of which we spotted a bit earlier) scattered about the vicinity. I believe he may have built much of the stonework in the chamber area but not the chamber itself.

Why don't we take the orange trail (north) and follow it over the boardwalk and through some swamp and then over the Bent Bridge? Back again on the wide gravel yellow-blazed path, we now have to find the dynamite storage shed site. For a small park, there sure is a lot to see around here. With our back to the Bent Bridge, face west and cross over the low stone wall in front of us. Walk about 50 feet in, with a little "English" to the left, and we'll come across a cleared, slightly raised rectangular area outlined with sand. This is the site of the dynamite storage shed (18 T 0604387, 4547756). The spur we discovered earlier came to the southern end of this site and is more visible when the leaves are down. The building had low, 2-foot-thick walls filled with the sand, which still remains after the building was disassembled. The walls supported a wood roof that would blow off if the dynamite exploded prematurely, the blast being contained and directed up by the walls. This was our last scheduled site for today, but I'm not done yet.

Because it's a nice day and we still have some energy left, I think what we'll do now is retrace back to the path, make a right turn (south) on the yellow trail and follow it back to the railroad grade intersection. We'll follow the grade in the direction of the crusher (left, or southeast), this time passing the massive foundation as the path turns to hiking tail (red-blazed) on its way to Hush Pond. The woods around here are somewhat muddy, usually very quiet (air traffic from Westchester Airport nearby as well as Metro North commuter trains do intrude from time to time) and extremely pleasant to hike through, with nominal elevation change. Once around Hush Pond (which is outside the preserve on White Plains

Watershed land), continue on red or any other trail we come across, in the direction of the nature center.

This route will bring us to old stone walls that go on and on, marking watershed boundaries. These impressive walls are being battered mercilessly by falling trees, which themselves are frequently being victimized by storms or hurricanes. Having no mortar or cement to hold them together, the walls lose. The red trail eventually becomes the Sunset Alley Trail (still red), which runs alongside the walls for its entire length, too soon bringing us back to our car.

8
DENNYTOWN MINES

WHERE: Fahnestock State Park, NY

WHY: Four iron mines, home site ruin, lonely millstone, site of Dennytown

DIFFICULTY: Moderate; 8 miles with frequent ascents and descents. No major elevation changes but many hills and some bushwhacking

MAP: New York–New Jersey Trail Conference Map, East Hudson Trails

UTM COORDINATES: Dennytown Mine: 18 T 0594994, 4586311
Mine off AT: 18 T 0590462, 4588155
Railroad bed at AT: 18 T 0596635, 4588129

DIRECTIONS: Taconic State Parkway north to Route 301 west, toward Cold Spring. Find Dennytown Road at about 3.5 miles down, and turn left (south). The second parking area, 1.1 miles in, is our start point. The stone utility shack off the road distinguishes the parking area. Look for the lonely ruin of an old stone lodging house just behind the shack, a bit set back into the field

The miles go by fairly painlessly on this marathon exploration, and the points of interest are nicely spaced apart to keep things interesting. This park has the most impressive grouping of iron mines and related sites on the east side of the Hudson that I can think of. Explore this park and save the toll on the Bear Mountain Bridge!

Dennytown itself is long gone. French settlers in the 1880s farmed the area and cut mines into the hillsides, extracting magnetite ore that wound up at, among other places, the West Point Foundry (remember that hike?) As we start off, heading northward on the blue-blazed Three Lakes Trail, we'll spot the clearing ahead

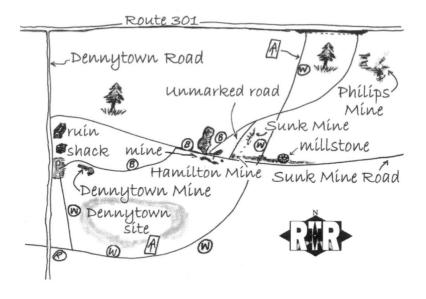

that looks like a swamp. That is the Dennytown site. Maybe foundations are in there, but I'm not willing to slog through mud and evade ticks to find out.

"So Dave," someone just asked, "why are we here?" Mines! We love mines, and this park has some that we just can't pass up. Barely a half-mile into the hike, we hit our first hill and begin to climb. After a short but steep climb through a narrow crevasse up to about 1,020 feet (we started at 820 feet), the blue trail tops out and bears sharply left near a tree with stones piled at its base. At this point look for the tailings pile (waste rock removed from the mine) and head in a general northerly direction to get to the beginning of the Dennytown Mine trench (18 T 0594994, 4586311). Follow the trench for about 40 feet, and it ends in an impressive circular pit of about 10 feet deep.

Continuing on the blue trail, we will soon cross Sunk Mine Road. Follow the blue blazes as it parallels the road and borders John Allen Pond. The trail crosses a stream near an attractive dam that acts as a spillway in high water. We can go to the edge of the pond for a fine (if early) lunch spot. Either way, after a short break along the water, go back to Sunk Mine Road and continue in the same direction as before (east).

Walking along the road, we'll come to another, smaller pond. Just as the pond comes into view, we should look for a car pullout on the left side of the road that goes to the water's edge. If we stand at that point, looking to the right we can see a faint trail heading off into the woods. Let's follow it to where a wall of rock ends the short trail at a "T." To the left and right runs a mine cut that isn't on the Trail Conference map. When our investigation of the cut is finished, we'll go back to the road and continue on our way.

At the end of the next bend, be on the lookout on our right for a notable homestead ruin. Stone walls mark the location from the road, and a somewhat brambly path is visible that leads us into the site. A well is up the short path on the left. A clearing soon opens to reveal walls that rise up surrounding a sunken area that shows where the house itself stood. Red tiles forming a patio of sorts are at the eastern end of the depression. Let's get back to the road; our next mine is just ahead.

Dave crossing a bridge.
Photo by Marcus Lieberman.

Down Sunk Mine Road a short distance, over a bridge crossing a stream is an unmarked trail on our left (north) side. The Hamilton Mine cut is a few steps up the road and off the trail, so look for the rock tailings that give the location away. This is surely one of the easiest mines to locate that I know of. The mine

Marcus by the trailhead ruin

is a narrow cut along a hillside and looks deep but flooded. All these mines are iron or magnetic iron: we are, after all, in a part of the iron-rich Ramapo Mountains/Hudson Highlands (they're close cousins).

We'll take the unmarked road northward. As we're walking on this trail, we'll come across infrequent, white-square blazes. Continuing north, at about 0.4 mile, our next target appears, heralded by an unusual sign:

DANGEROUS CONDITIONS
ABSOLUTELY NO ACCESS TO THIS AREA PERMITTED
New York State Office of Parks,
Recreation and Historic Preservation
Taconic Region Staatsburg, NY 12580

Well then, we'd better stay out. If we continued past the sign on the faint trail worn into the rock, just over the ridge we'd probably see the huge Sunk Mine cut on the hillside far below. One imagines it would be a long, painful fall down onto those hard, sharp rocks if we were foolish enough to get too close to the edge.

I should state, at this point, that the Trail Conference map is absolutely correct in regards to where it pinpoints all the mines we're looking for today.

The unmarked road continues northeasterly past the Sunk Mine and then becomes indistinct. We'll bear left at a rock face just past the mine. Look for cut deadfall to locate the path, which bends in a northwesterly direction and narrows to a footpath, sometimes with those white squares pointing the way. Without warning, the blue-blazed Three Lakes Trail junction appears, and we're back on track.

From this point, our trail follows the blue blazes through the laurel for 2.5 miles. Continue past the Appalachian Trail junction. At a point one-half mile before meeting up with Route 301 we'll pass the remains of the Philips Mine, a series of mossy tailings piles, trenches, and cuts that parallel the path. It's interesting to investigate the site, but we keep looking for some big feature that just isn't here. Just before encountering Route 301 bear left (southwest) on a dirt path for 0.2 mile and pick up the Appalachian Trail as it heads to the left (SSE) into the woods. Once we pass the trail register, things pick up again.

The AT follows the former right-of-way of a narrow gauge, mule-powered railroad. The beasts pulled ore-laden cars from the Sunk and Canada Mines up to a point near Route 301 on this track. (The Canada mine is near Pelton Pond, and one opening is visible off Route 301 just west of the Pelton Pond picnic area.) Following the railroad bed can be entertaining as we look for rock blasting drill marks in the craggy face to our right (west). Some remarkable grades and fills keep our attention as we go along.

We'll stay on the AT as it drops through swampy hemlock stands and ascends toward fine mountaintop viewpoints across the valley to Candlewood Hill (eastward). Before that, though, there is an impressive "unmarked" mine cut that we need to check out while we're here.

As the trail drops through the hemlock, be aware of a point at which the stream on our left expands into a swampy area. The apparent remains of a railroad bed are on the right (18 T 0596635, 4588129), just past thick briars we passed through on the AT. We will turn right (SE) and follow the bed to the short tailings pile of black rock we see just ahead. Tailings, also called overburden, is waste rock that has been removed from the mine opening and dumped nearby. Learning to recognize tailings is a major way to locate hidden iron mines, as well as finding the old roads that will frequently lead us to them. Up on the hillside is more spilled overburden, which we'll *very carefully* climb. Some of the rock up here is alarmingly loose as we scramble to the top. Once up, the impressive 150-foot-long (or so) mine cut (18 T 0596462, 4588155) reveals a sharp 40-foot drop down to the flooded shaft below. There are a few other holes and cuts to examine uphill from here, but extreme caution must be taken when scrambling around to prevent potentially fatal slips on the loose rock and dirt. The wide mine opening is right below us.

After a careful descent, we're back on the AT. This part of the park has a remote and primitive feel to it that is very pleasant to experience. Shortly before the trail meets Sunk Mine Road, a wooden footbridge crosses a lively cascade. A sign to our left states:

AREA CLOSED
WILDLIFE HABITAT RECOVERY AREA
DO NOT ENTER
THANK YOU

If we followed the cascade downstream some yards to a point where the falls slacken off, we'd find a complete but broken mill-stone sitting in the still water among the rocks. The last 1.5 miles of the AT will get us 1,061 feet up before the trail dips and we return to our starting point. Beware of the red Catfish Loop Trail, because the AT makes a sharp right-hand turn toward the parking area at that point. We'll pass through some old Dennytown stone walls as we finish up, and we'll get another close view of the town clearing.

Nice day in the woods. We deserve some dinner in historic Cold Spring. Come to think of it, the West Point Foundry hike is over there . . .

Millstone

9
DOODLETOWN

WHERE: Harriman State Park, NY

WHY: Town site, foundations, abandoned stairways, two mines, two cemeteries, old roads

DIFFICULTY: Moderate; about 6 miles round-trip, with some hills and a climb to the Doodletown Mine

MAP: New York–New Jersey Trail Conference Map, Harriman/Bear Mountain Trails

UTM COORDINATES: Doodletown Mine: 18 T 0583356, 4571655
Mine Road at trail: 18 T 0583589, 4571893
Edison Mine: 18 T 0584458, 4571761

DIRECTIONS: Palisades Parkway north to the traffic circle near the Bear Mountain Bridge. At the traffic circle, take Route 9W south. The hiker's parking area is about 1.4 miles south of the Bear Mountain Bridge traffic circle on Route 9W, just before the road into Iona Island

There are few standing ruins left at Doodletown. What makes this hike interesting is the human history associated with the area, along with some scattered remains of yesteryear: stairs to nowhere, foundations of long-gone residences, an elusive iron mine hidden on the north flank of West Mountain, Thomas Edison's experimental mine, and the two historic cemeteries that are still in use. Photographic opportunities abound. Doodletown is a genuine ghost town, vintage 1965.

The great thing about hiking in Doodletown is that there is always something more to see next time. I've been exploring the

99

area for years and continue to come up with new discoveries. Foundations and wells still lurk amid the sharp barberry bushes.

At the hikers' parking area, we'll cross 9W and pick up the blue-blazed trail near the sign for the merry-go-round (at the Bear Mountain Inn) to the right of the brook. The path makes a steep 100-foot climb on decayed blacktop before leveling off near the foundation of the Gray home. This area was known, appropriately enough, as "Gray's Hill." A number of foundations and stairways are on both sides of the trail as we make our way to the reservoir, dam, and second schoolhouse sites.

Ancestors of the June family, Huguenot in origin, first settled in the area in the mid-1700s. According to the *Walk Book,* the name of the town may stem from the Dutch, who first encountered the area after a fire and named it "Dood dell," or "dead valley." English settlers added the "town" suffix in later years. Some well-known Doodletown families included the Jones, Stalter, Herbert, Youmans, and June families; area landmarks such as Jones Point carry on their legacy. The men of Doodletown worked through the years at the nearby iron mine, on road building projects in the area, and as grape pickers on Iona Island in the Hudson River.

Doodletown was the last parcel of land to be acquired by the Palisades Interstate Park Commission as it formed Harriman State Park and Bear Mountain State Park. The commission generously offered the families the option of accepting fair market value for their homes if they agreed to sell or face the threat of seizure by eminent domain if they refused. One by one, bit by bit, everyone sold. The final parcel of land to be acquired, finally ending more than two hundred years of the little town's existence, took place in 1965.

Many descendants of the dispossessed Doodletowners still live in nearby towns such as Fort Montgomery.

We eventually meet up with the 1777E trail, one of the four Bicentennial commemorative trails in the park (1777 east and west, 1779, and Anthony Wayne). We'll do the history lesson a little later when we get deeper into the town site. Wide Lemmon Road comes in and heads to the right, passing the former tree nursery, concrete capped reservoir, and the ski trail that passes by the first June cemetery sites, but we aren't doing that today.

The interpretive signs that are posted around are relatively new and take the guesswork out of our explorations. My only complaint, however minor, is that these helpful signs intrude on our photography. I wish they'd have been placed a little farther from the features they explain.

We soon come to a "T" intersection, with a sign pointing out:

← JUNE CEMETERY
HISTORIC SITES →

We'll bear to the left and respectfully inspect the second, relocated June cemetery. The first was on a rise above Gray's Hill, and signs near the Lemmon Road intersection will bring the adventurous hiker there if there's interest, although nothing but a marker remains at the site. Flags and flowers remind us that this is still an active burial ground, and the diminutive cherubs marking some graves are poignant. On one recent visit, a large, black rat snake was soaking up some sun in a bush beside the road. Copperheads and rattlers are also known to be in the area.

It's time to retrace our steps and head 0.3 mile in the direction that the sign pointed to the "historic sites." At the wide intersection of Doodletown Road and Pleasant Valley Road (beautiful downtown Doodletown), we'll take a short break and check out the map posted there. The red posted numbers we encounter as we nose around are ski trail identifiers. Elevation here is at about 280 feet.

More interpretive signs mark long-gone properties. How sad that the little village was made to disappear. I'm sure that by now, if Doodletown were still around, some enterprising villager would be selling ice cream and hamburgers in the summer and hot chocolate in the winter to hungry hikers.

Following the 1777E trail south, it soon splits when the '77W heads west as it circles Bear Mountain. For now, we'll pick up the '77W and follow it through the woods and over a brook on a wooden bridge as it gently climbs up to a point where it meets Doodletown Road and the yellow-blazed Suffern–Bear Mountain Trail. We did this so we can now follow Doodletown Road to the east and downhill, passing a part of the old town that once had many residences. Some remnants, however, await our attention.

The Bambino home site is marked by an interpretive sign and iron rails embedded in the path. You may find a home site and foundation at the top of the hill. We'll encounter additional foundations and more steps to missing homes as we approach the signed "District #7" school site, where there once stood a large stone structure that became the pride of the town. The church site is just a few steps down. After Doodletown was abandoned in the mid-1960s, the park used the various standing buildings, schools, and churches as garages and residences for workers. Decay and vandalism forced razing of the structures, such as the school, in the late 1980s.

Arriving back at the Pleasant Valley Road, we'll again bear south, this time passing the '77W intersection but soon coming to the signed entrance to the Herbert Cemetery, the older of the two graveyards we'll explore today. It is still active, and some area

Steps to a vanished Doodletown home

Herbert cemetery

Mark at the church ruin

people have permits that allow them to drive in. Look around; there is a fascinating mix of historic and modern gravestones here.

Continuing south on the '77, paths and steps are everywhere. Long gone are any homes or structures, but the Thomas property (identified by a sign) has a ruin on the hill just above the path.

At 0.3 mile past the Herbert Cemetery, a ski trail, marked by another map/number board, crosses our route. This is a good spot to take a break and talk history for a bit as we look for redcoat footprints in the soil.

On October 6, 1777, two thousand British troops under Sir Henry Clinton marched north from Stony Point, briefly occupying Doodletown. After a short skirmish with a small group of Continental soldiers, they headed north and then divided into two columns, now the commemorative 1777 East and West trails. One column circled Bear Mountain to the west and attacked Fort Montgomery (north of what now is the Bear Mountain Bridge). The eastern column attacked Fort Clinton (where the bridge is today), gaining control of that section of the Hudson River.

Face south. Look up to your left (southeasterly) through the trees and identify the cleft summit of Dunderburg Mountain. Although identified on the trail map both as Bald and Dunderburg mountains, it's actually just Dunderburg with two peaks. To our right across the valley is West Mountain, which sports an historic shelter on the south end and an impressive iron mine on the north side that we'll visit a little later. Pleasant Valley lies straight ahead of us between the two peaks.

Continuing south on the 1777 trail will soon bring us to a pair of spruce trees flanking a paved path (on the right). Walk down this road for a few steps and see the small, deep cellar hole of John Stalter Jr.'s home. There are other house sites down this path but little to actually discover. Look for an ornamental Osage orange tree that's in the vicinity. Nature has reclaimed this part of Doodletown.

Back on the path and turn right (south). The pavement ends and sometimes becomes flooded by Timp Brook. At 0.6 mile from the intersection of the ski trail, on the left, we arrive at the remnants of the Moore property. Originally a residence that was later a children's summer camp run by Riverside Church in New York City, the camp operated from 1932 to 1953. Previous versions of the New York–New Jersey Trail Conference map for Harriman State Park list the still-standing garage as a shelter. The latest reprint does not.

This is also a fine lunch spot. When the cascade is running, it is quite pleasant to linger along the bank and think of the once-vital village that used to exist here. This is a popular destination, however, and on weekends we will most likely have to share our quiet place with other hikers or overnight campers.

Some great features still await our presence, so let's get going. Backtracking northward on the '77, when we get to the ski trail intersection let's pause for a moment and check out the Scandell home foundation, once again marked by a sign. Heading up the short hill on an obvious path brings us to an impressive house foundation and water pump base.

Back at the ski trail intersection, it's time to hit the mine, a highlight of the trip as far as I'm concerned. Following the ski trail 0.3 mile west from the Pleasant Valley Road intersection will bring us to the mine road on our left (the south side of the trail), which is a few yards before a small wooden footbridge over a stream (use18 T 0583589, 4571893 to find it). Looking carefully, we'll see the mine road joining the ski trail at about a 45-degree angle to the right (in other words, it is not at a right angle to the trail). The old mine

Todd at Doodletown Mine

road can be a challenge to follow as it sweeps to the left around a knoll, crosses the brook, and follows cairns in a generally southwestward direction toward the mine.

This mine can be tricky to locate, so please don't feel bad if you have trouble finding it. Usually we begin looking out for the mine road or some tailings (also known as overburden which is rock removed from the mine and usually dumped downhill), but the trail up can sometimes be indistinct. Trust the Trail Conference map; it places the mine perfectly. Luckily this time out we have a good leader who follows the cairns marking the mine road up to a point where the black tailings pile suddenly presents itself to us intrepid mine-hunters. Success! Climbing to the left of the tailings dump and then turning to the right once on top, we finally get to check out the mysterious Doodletown Mine (18 T 0583356, 4571655) just past a fire pit.

SPECIAL NOTE TO HIKE LEADERS:
Be prepared and bring a strong magnet with you for this part of the trip. Check the dark gray rocks in the mine dump vicinity for magnetic attraction. Get your compass out and wave some ore around it to see how the different poles on each side of the tailing affects the needle rotation. I dropped my magnet into the tailings pile and it came out absolutely covered with iron material, attracting large ore-laden chunks with a satisfying clank.

The mine is a long trench cut into the hillside, flooded at the far end where it widens out and descends into the vein. It was most likely an iron mine active in the 1800s, and quite probably even before that, during the early days of the town. Sitting at about 630 feet up and surrounded by forest and running water, it's a natural spot to take a break. After careful exploration, let's return to the ski trail, passing Pleasant Valley Road as we make our way to our next mine. Doodletown Mine is quite excellent and you *will* want to return here. Guaranteed.

After we walk 0.7 mile through forest down the wide ski trail, the Edison Mine (18 T 0584458, 4571761) awaits us up a hill on the right side (east) of the trail, just a few tenths of a mile southeast of the June cemetery and reservoir dam. It's a large circular cut, betrayed, as usual, by the black rock dump spilling down below it.

Thomas A. Edison had an experimental magnetic ore separation technique, and this was an early attempt to find an iron vein on land he owned in order to test the process. In later years he used his separator at the Sunk Mine in Fahnestock State Park, the Sterling (Forest) mines, and also at a larger plant near Ogdensburg, NJ, that processed the iron into round "cakes" (instead of the more traditional "pigs"), using yet another process he developed. The cut didn't yield much iron; our compass and magnet verify that.

After our mine inspection, continuing along brings us by the Caldwell Turnpike intersection as that old road bears eastward. Although we aren't going down that way, it's worth pointing out that the notable ruin of a church sits on the left side of the trail about a quarter-mile down. The road is in extremely bad condition, and once you find the site, all those thorny barberry bushes thickly surrounding the crumbling walls can make inspection very unpleasant.

After this intersection, we cross a concrete bridge that spans a lively waterfall. The pooling waters down below the falls were known to those long-ago Doodletown children as the "Ten Foot," a favorite local swimming hole. In short order we come back to the broken asphalt of the 1777 East trail.

The '77E goes straight uphill toward Fort Clinton, but unlike the British, we're turning right and retracing the old road back to our car and the modern world.

10
DUNDERBURG SPIRAL RAILWAY

We have plenty to see on this trip, with the star attractions being the features associated with the Dunderburg Spiral Railway. Back in the 1870s, Mr. Henry J. Mumford successfully operated a tourist switchback railroad, originally used to haul coal out of the mountains, in Maunch Chunk, PA (now Jim Thorpe, PA) and decided to try it here for the delight of hard-working New Yorkers. It was intended to have been drawn up by cable to the top of Dunderburg Mountain and gravity-fed in a spiral, meandering path back down to a tunnel at Route 9W. Construction began in 1890, but the project was abruptly

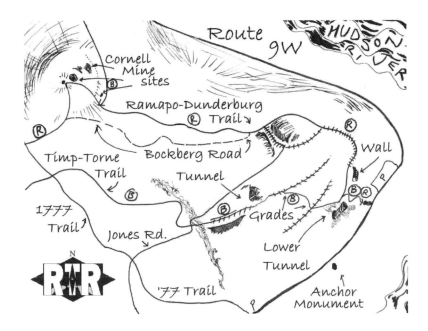

stopped in 1891 because of a recession. After an investment of about a year's work and a million dollars, all there was to show for the laborers' hard work were the astounding constructions that we will discover on this hike. You'll need to bring the Big Flashlight.

The Timp-Torne (blue blaze) and Ramapo-Dunderburg (red blaze) trails meet Route 9W a few yards south of the sign. Following primarily the blue Timp-Torne Trail, we'll begin our adventure. Minutes in, we'll see a stonework tunnel buried in the woods to the left. This was to have been where the railway cars ended up after the excursion down the mountain (think of it as a carport rather than a tunnel). Investigate the tunnel, and then go back to the T-T and begin climbing in earnest.

This can be a challenging hike. Fortunately, there are numerous rewards for our hard work. Along this section of the trail there are many opportunities to rest and look out high over the Hudson River and across it to the embattled Indian Point nuclear power plant in Buchanan.

In a tough half-mile or so from the tunnel, we will begin to see the railway cuts and rights of way more clearly. We finally level off at 612 feet and follow a grade to the left (southwesterly). After a few minutes of tracing the old rail bed, look to your right—now *that's* what I call a tunnel! Take a minute, break out that flashlight and do an inspection. This tunnel was supposed to have been cut all the way through the rock but remains unfinished and is frequently mistaken for a cave by those who know less than we do.

Continue southerly on the Timp-Torne for 0.1 mile, admiring the mighty rail bed as we go. We now come to a stream crossing and a woods road on the other side. The T-T continues to go straight ahead and up. At this point, before crossing the stream, we can circle around to our right and see the other side of the unfinished tunnel.

Cross over the water and go to the intersection of the woods road and the T-T. Bear right (northerly) on the unblazed woods road. This is the Jones Trail, actually a service road for the railway during construction. Follow the Jones (unmarked) up, up, up to where it meets with a right of way. Turn left (west) and follow the trail through the cut. This is a remarkable section of the railway. If you weren't sure you were following a rail bed earlier, you must be sure now. Okay, now step back in time 110 or so years and imagine you are in an

Lower tunnel

Upper tunnel

open rail car, gently gliding through this section. The Big City is a hundred miles away . . .

After walking peacefully for a bit, we come across the Ramapo-Dunderburg Trail (red). Bear left (west) and follow it, taking care not to mistakenly take the unmarked woods road that appears on the left a few yards down. That is the Bockberg Road, a woods road that we will encounter again later in the hike.

For now, we leave the scenic spiral railway and start hiking on the R-D toward our next destination, the Cornell iron mine. The trail climbs steadily to the top of Dunderburg Mountain but is gracious enough to pass some high ledges with great views of Bear Mountain, the Hudson River, and the valley below. We'll do the formal tour at the top.

The Cornell Trail (blue) comes in from the right at 0.8 mile after the rail bed intersection. Let's start looking for mine sites now. Turning right (north) on the Cornell, there are two mine trenches on the left-hand side of the trail as you descend, identified by tailings piles. Find the first one, and about 200 feet lower is the second, also on the left. I include these here only in the spirit of completeness; I'd choose to avoid the steep uphill backtrack, saving my energy for the other Cornell sites that are more interesting.

At the intersection of the Cornell and Ramapo-Dunderburg is a large exploratory pit. Stay on the R-D, ascending for a short distance until it bears left. Look carefully on your right for a faint path and a cairn, next to a blazed tree (18 T 0584553, 4570851). Follow the level contour of the mountain to your right for about 150 feet, looking for a large tailings pile. Climb the tailings and check out the horizontal tunnel (or "adit") of the Cornell Mine (18 T 0584489, 4570871). It's about 5 feet high by 50 feet deep and usually water-filled. I've seen all sorts of small critters in here and a nest with bird eggs once. Owing to flooding and debris, the adit is not enterable, but it's still an impressive visual and you'll want your Big Light.

Look above the tunnel slightly to your right, and you will see another tailings pile with another mine site worth investigating. These mines were worked sometime around 1859.

Returning to the R-D, climb up to the peak of Bald Mountain (although technically still Dunderburg, because there are two sum- mits). There is a deep vertical shaft near the point where the trail makes a sharp right toward the rocky summit (on the east side of the trail, a few feet downhill). Do check it out with extreme caution. Then get over to the lookout (1,120 feet) and take in that view.

Let us lunch on the rocky top while we survey our domain. To the north is the Bear Mountain Bridge, with Anthony's Nose above the eastern anchorage. There are various stories about this place name, but it is not in honor of the great general "Mad" Anthony Wayne; this Anthony apparently was a musician in the Continental Army who had a large nose. Follow the bridge to the western side. Just north is Fort Montgomery and south is the site of Fort Clinton, two Revolution-era forts captured by the British in 1777. Do you see the stone tower on top of the mountain straight across the val- ley? Perkins Memorial Tower sits on top of Bear Mountain. George W. Perkins Sr. was the first chairman of the Palisades Interstate Park Commission, from 1900 to 1920. In the valley below us and slightly forward sits the abandoned hamlet of Doodletown (I *know* you've done that hike with us), and Iona Island is on the right. To our extreme left (west) is West Mountain. There is a scenic hiking shelter on the south side of West Mountain and an iron mine at the north end.

Continue now on the R-D (in the same direction we've been hiking) for 0.4 mile downhill, where an unmarked woods road comes in on our left. That would be the other end of the Bockberg Road. Take the Bockberg, and when in doubt, as the trail occasionally appears to split, stay to the right on the widest path. Don't let that frighten you because it really isn't tough to follow. Take it. We might see ruts in the mud from the park rangers' patrols.

We'll soon return to the junction of Bockberg Road and Ramapo-Dunderburg Trail that we noted earlier today. Bear right (east) on the R-D, and follow it all the way back to the parking lot. It climbs through the tall grass for a while before beginning a wild downhill drop, passing numerous (thorny) ripe wild raspberry bushes in the summer and equally pervasive wild blueberry bushes that both offer hikers a quick snack.

The R-D was recently relocated to take advantage of the Spiral Railway grades, and we will once more walk on near-completed cuts and features of the rail. Witness the large freestanding cutstone wall that we walk past. Grades aside, it is the last "new" vestige of the Railway that we will come upon today. The R-D joins with the blue Timp-Torne we hiked up earlier today, and we take the path back downhill (to the left) to Route 9W. Once back at the car, stretch, change out of your hiking shoes, and plan on a hot shower and medication tonight. This was a tough hike!

11
GREAT CAMP SANTANONI

WHERE: Newcomb, NY

WHY: An abandoned Great Camp in the Adirondacks and primitive campsites beside a lake

DIFFICULTY: Moderate; about 10 miles round-trip, with a gentle 200-foot elevation change

MAP: Farm site map and lodge area map, available (sometimes) at the Visitor Center in Newcomb

UTM COORDINATES: Delia Spring: 18 T 0569386, 4874295

WEBSITE: www.aarch.org/html/santanoni/history.html

BROCHURE: A Brief Guide to Camp Santanoni

DIRECTIONS: New York State Thruway (I-87) north to exit 29 (Route 2 west). Take Route 2 west to Route 28N west into Newcomb.

The main lodge of abandoned Camp Santanoni is our primary objective this time out.

Some of the best primitive campsites on the face of the earth are located along Newcomb Lake in the Santanoni Preserve, just before the lodge. I suggest that you take advantage of the camping and do this exploration as a backpacking trip. Bring a good hurricane lamp.

Avoid this hike during black fly season, mid-May to late June; during the day the swarming, tiny, biting monsters will make the trip unbearable as they look for a hot meal at your expense, and the equally annoying mosquitoes will snack on you at night.

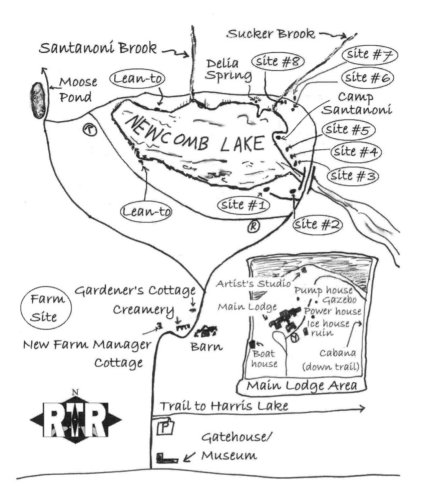

We will begin with a stop at the Adirondack Visitors Center on Route 28N in Newcomb. Ask for the *Camp Santanoni* brochure as well as the campsite and farm site maps, in addition to whatever else they might have regarding the old camp.

Turn left out of the visitor center parking lot (east). There are signs to the Santanoni Preserve parking lot a few miles down on Route 28N. After parking in the upper lot, you will see a trail pointing toward Lake Harris, but don't take it. Instead, there is a gated dirt road that we will take up to the camp. Before we do that, though, walk down to the gatehouse, which has a small museum, and start your Great Camp research here. In season, this is where we would find out about tours through the camp.

Begin the hike by proceeding north on Newcomb Road (the dirt road), past the trail register. Be sure to sign in. The state gauges trail use that way and it's also a safety issue. The route is clearly signed; the road is wide, mostly level, and easy to follow.

In about a mile we arrive at the farm site, which is our first ruin. As quickly as possible, pull out that farm site map that we scored at the visitors center and let's see what's what. The two most important structures were the huge storybook barn on our right and the stone-arched creamery to the left. (Careless smokers caused a fire that destroyed the historic barn in early July 2004.) The last house on the left as we continue in is a Sears "kit" house that predates the Great Camp period.

I've been told that once you cross the first stone bridge past the farm site, the ruin of a maple syrup "sugar house" is a few yards to the left of the path (following a stream uphill), but repeated searching of the area has made me believe there is nothing left to see at the site. At 2.5 miles, a trail comes in on the left. It heads through the woods another 5 or so miles toward Moose Pond, where a boathouse once existed.

The hiking is easy as we make our way to the old camp. A red trail appears on our left as we close in. That trail circles Newcomb Lake and accesses the first of two lean-tos; the other is off of the yellow trail that intersects with red on the other side of the lake.

There are eight primitive campsites dotted along the eastern side of Newcomb Lake, and let's not forget the two lean-tos flanking the lake further west. Closer to the camp itself, campsites #1 and #5 are the pick, in my opinion. Site #1 is the most remote and has an outhouse, but no picnic table. It also has a small, sandy beach on the lake shore. Nice! Sites #3, #4, and #5 have outhouses and picnic tables, are roomy, and are nicely isolated from the world. Site #8 is a large group site. I can't prove this, but I suspect that some of the folks who are currently working at Santanoni have held some pretty good parties at this one (the makeshift bar I saw there is the tip-off). The other sites (#2, #6, and #7) are less attractive and are right off the hiking trail that circles the lake, thereby affording little sense of privacy in their isolation. Sometimes picnic tables are there, but on my last visit there weren't any tables at sites #6 or #7.

Before we properly explore the Great Camp, let's drop our packs at site #2 and have lunch beside the lake. Fueled and ready, it's time to cross over the wooden bridge and head down the road toward Great Camp Santanoni.

We don't see the big house until we are right on top of it. I'll withhold a detailed description because the initial discovery is the key to a proper first impression.

This is a magnificent place. On the other side of the house is a flight of steps that lead downhill to a small clearing that affords a wide view of the calm lake and cloud-ringed mountains that surround it. The artist's studio, just to the right of the main building, has expansive views of Newcomb Lake through wide, arched windows. The large, reconstructed boathouse is to the left of the lodge, and some other fallen buildings lie near the main yellow trail that

cuts through the site. A restored blue cabana sits beside a small beach just down the trail, past the lodge and before the last few campsites.

Delia Spring (and its supposed restorative qualities) supplied water to the main house via pipeline and is located on the north shore of Newcomb Lake about a quarter-mile past Sucker Brook (by campsite #8). The spring is far easier to locate by boat from the lake: Follow

Back of the lodge

Looking toward the boathouse

Artist's studio

Boathouse, before its reconstruction

the continuous shoreline from campsite #8 until you come upon a "thumb" of land sticking out into the lake. Delia Spring is on the other side, where the shoreline resumes. To find it, look and listen for the magical spring water flowing out of a pipe, just above the water level. It can be covered with grass or moss, making it tricky to locate, but you can hear it when you get close enough. Clear the debris away from the pipe and fill up those jugs. Whenever I mentioned to locals that I was looking for Delia Spring (18 T 0569386, 4874295), they all wished me luck finding the Fountain of Youth.

The first time I came here was during a spring 2002 backpacking trip with RTR operative Todd. It was a miserably raw, cold, wet day, and most of it was spent establishing our campsite. It wasn't until nighttime that we were first able to explore the main house. He had a flashlight, and I used a small Dietz Comet hurricane lamp. We were able to go into some unlocked rooms and used only the flickering lamplight to navigate through the lodge. This is good stuff.

The big house is quiet, lonely, and elegant after dark, not menacing at all. It may not fully understand why someone would want to abandon it. The reason why is best told around our campfire tonight.

The 1890s were the beginning of a time when wealthy families
built Adirondack Great Camps, which are large, rustic-style vacation estates. White Pine Camp and Camp Sagamore are two of the
better-known camps, and both are open for tours in the summer.
Over thirty of these Great Camps were known to have existed.
Robert Pruyn (pronounced "prine") was a well-connected Albany
businessman who had amassed close to 13,000 acres near Newcomb. He began building Camp Santanoni in 1892 and completed it
by the following year. It was among the first of these Great Camps,
and architecturally it was probably the best regarded. At the peak of
its existence, Camp Santanoni was entirely self-supporting by way
of a large farm that provided meat, milk, and greens, and the sur-
plus was sold in local area markets.

Camp Santanoni does not have the huge buildings or bowling
alleys sometimes associated with Great Camps such as Sagamore. What it does have is its own unique style. There are many
differently designed groups of buildings that survived the abandonment. The six-bedroom gatehouse has a classical stone arch
entrance. The farm complex site is notable for its expansive size,
native stone buildings, and a European look—until thoughtless
fools torched the barn. The main lodge is actually six separate
buildings with a common roof and porch done in Adirondack rus-
tic style. When seen from above, the roofline suggests a symbolic
phoenix in flight, which was an influence from the days when
Robert's father was U.S. ambassador to Japan, from 1862 to 1865
under Abraham Lincoln.

The Melvin family of Syracuse bought Camp Santanoni in 1953.
They lived and played there into the 1970s, on a somewhat reduced
grand scale. In 1971, their eight-year-old cousin, Douglas Legg, and
his father were walking through the property when dad told Douglas to go back to the house and put on long pants for poison ivy
protection (there is no poison ivy present in the Adirondacks). The
boy disappeared on his way back to the lodge and was never seen
again. A massive manhunt lasting over a week was launched in a
frantic attempt to locate him, but no trace was ever found.

Devastated by this tragic event, the Melvins sold the camp, and
it eventually became state property through various land deals.

Except for occasional hunters or campers staying overnight, the old camp has stood abandoned and vacant in the woods since that time.

Camp Santanoni became part of the New York State Forest Preserve in 1972. Most of the original estate had become part of the High Peaks Wilderness Area, while the rest went to the Vanderwacker Mountain Wild Forest. In 2000, the Camp Santanoni Historic Area was created to protect 32 acres of the old camp, the farm site, and the road in. It is also a National Historic Landmark as of 2000.

Presently there is a restoration project going on, and occasional guided tours will go through the lodge. During the summer you can take a horse-pulled wagon into Camp Santanoni. Some people put their canoes on the wagon and use them on Newcomb Lake. During a summer day it can be a busy place, with hikers, bikers, canoers, and day-trippers on horse-pulled wagons all sharing the road on the way to explore Santanoni.

Tonight, however, we're camping beside the lake, and after the day people leave, we have this tranquil wooded place all to ourselves. We can build our campfire and cook a nice dinner while we drink the water we bottled earlier today from the Fountain of Youth. After dark we'll let the fire burn down, grab our hurricane lamps, and then go out and explore the place again . . .

12
HARRIMAN RUINS IN WINTER

WHERE: Harriman State Park, NY

WHY: Quality ruins-hunting when park access is limited: two mansion sites, mysterious stone chamber, iron mine, historic cemetery, fire tower, hiker's shelter

DIFFICULTY: Moderate to challenging, depending on the route we choose

MAP: New York–New Jersey Trail Conference Map, Southern Harriman/ Bear Mountain Trails

UTM COORDINATES:
Hasenclever Road at Lake Welch Drive: 18 T 0577382, 4565621
Turnoff to stone chamber: 18 T 0577227, 4566208
Stone chamber: 18 T 0577245, 4566161

DIRECTIONS: Palisades Parkway north to exit 14, Willow Grove Road/ Route 98. Take 98 west to the junction of Gate Hill Road/Route 106. Continue west for 0.3 mile to a large parking area on the left at a gated road by a yellow-blazed trail.

When the winter season shuts down some of the roads in Harriman State Park, thereby limiting where we can legally leave a car, a little ingenuity can help us satisfy our ruins-finding itch when our customary favorite parking spots are closed. The area adjoining Lake Welch Beach and Beaver Pond Campground is worth saving for the cold weather. It has plenty of worthwhile sites to investigate when winter and snow tangle up our chapter-following plans for other sites in the park.

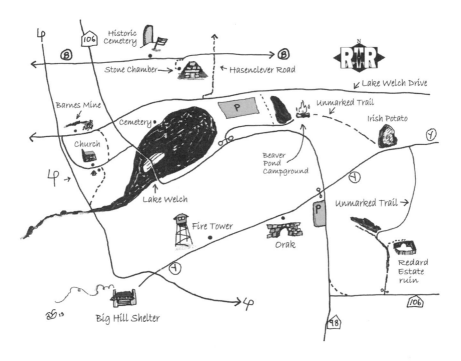

The situation here is that there's so much to get to that doing it all in one short winter day would be exhausting and impractical, so instead I'm going to lay out one huge marathon hike, and you can pick and choose the sites any way you like.

To see everything, we can bisect it thusly:

Loop A *(easier, about 5 miles)*: Parking lot, Redard site, chamber, cemetery, back through Lake Welch to the car

Loop B *(challenging, about 7 miles)*:Lake Welch Beach, chamber, cemetery, Barnes Mine, Big Hill Shelter, fire tower, and Orak

We'll be hiking a big, spoked wheel, counterclockwise, the different access points noted, with the spokes representing the various access or exit trails. Make sure you bring multiple light sources with you (including a headlight) on winter hikes and be well aware of when darkness sets in: typically around 4:30 P.M. on the shortest days, so you want to be out by 4 P.M. Daylight can slip away faster than expected when you're busy exploring, and you do not want to be finding your way back in the dark, snow, and ice.

There were two sizable estates in this area that left us with remains to investigate: the little-visited Redard home we're going to see right now and the more-visited Orak site at the other end of the hike. More about Orak later.

Beginning Loop A: Starting from the parking area on Route 106 just east of Lake Welch, our first decision is how to get to the Redard estate ruin. To avoid backtracking, we can head downhill (eastward) on Route 106 and then left (north) on Gate Hill Road to a point where the old broken-blacktopped Redard driveway terminates at a wire-rope gate opposite Blanchard Road, a distance of about a mile on an active street. We don't love hiking on asphalt, but sometimes it's the only way. Once we get to it, we can pick up the driveway and get off the street, heading steadily uphill to where it levels off, and we'll soon see the stone walls of Redard to our right, a bit more uphill. Take note that the trail we'll follow after we're done here continues ahead and then downhill.

The remains of the sizable Rose O. Redard property include the barberry- and vine-overgrown home site and a walled enclosure with its stone-arched entrance that is still intact. There is a small rock-enclosed pool (possibly a tiny fish pond) at the eastern side of the garden and plenty of remnants of outbuildings to discover as we walk the perimeter of the garden wall. Electrical conduits, various plumbing, a boiler, and plenty more artifacts are at the site.

Redard estate

I've been told this property is somehow linked to Red Rose Tea, but the history page at the Canada-based company's website doesn't mention Rose, any family named "Redard," or any connection to New York.

Once done at Redard, it's time to move on, keeping the short winter day in mind. Backtracking to the point where we left the driveway, the wide gravel road heads downhill to a quiet lake favored by local fishermen. Although the road continues straight ahead, where it meets the lake, we'll be careful not to follow it but to bear right (northeastward), crossing an outlet and stream, picking up the sometimes-faint, unmarked trail that skirts the north side of the water. The path follows the lake for a short distance before heading northwesterly and uphill into the woods. If we make a mistake and do not turn off at the junction, the road on the south side of the water will soon dead-end, a tip-off that we missed our crossing.

The trail that we're looking for on the north side of the lake is not widely used or heavily trampled and can be challenging to pick out: in my experience, it's easier to follow it traveling eastward (but if you do that on this hike, you'll have to backtrack).

NOTE TO HIKE LEADERS:

It might be prudent to scout this section in warmer weather before leading people here, and forming a GPS track may well save you some stressful moments when you're traveling in the opposite direction for the first time.

After exploring the estate ruin and then finding the trail that leads us out, within the hour we'll wind up on the yellow-blazed Suffern–Bear Mountain trail, where we'll turn left (east), climbing to high views while passing by plentiful glacial erratics and glacier-scoured rock faces. At the Irish Potato, a huge erratic, an unmarked but recognizable side trail heads off to the right into the Beaver Pond Campground, which is a good spot for lunch or a map-study break before continuing the adventure.

Beaver Pond can be a good camping base for this hike during

"shoulder" season, if we do it then, but it gets very busy, crowded, and noisy here at the height of the summer. Because you've back-packed to the peaceful solitude of a spot such as the campsites at Great Camp Santanoni (see that chapter) it's totally understandable that you'd not be happy here during the crush. Other, more accept-able camping opportunities will come our way a little later on.

(If you're doing Loop B, you started at the car, headed toward Beaver Pond Campground, and wound up somewhere in this vicin-ity.) We need to get over to the causeway in front of us that runs between Lake Welch and the pond, and follow it past the deserted beach with its vacant vending stands and frozen lake to the large parking lot at the other side of the complex. Our next key junction is the point where the unmarked Hasenclever Road meets Lake Welch Drive. We'll need to carefully follow our trail map, because it's a bit tricky to find. We'll head to the right of the picnic area, passing through the parking lot, and get to Lake Welch Drive, where we bear left and look for the point where the Hasenclever curves down-hill and meets the road (18 T 0577382, 4565621). Loop A and Loop B continue.

Taking the old woods road, which continues to the fine Hasen-clever Mine site (worthwhile, hard to resist, but not today), at about 0.4 mile the blue Beech Trail crosses and we'll pick it up, heading to the left (west). In a fairly short distance, maybe a few tenths of a mile, there is a large boulder with a blue blaze (18 T 0577227, 4566208). This is an old farm site; our mysterious stone chamber is buried in the overgrowth. We do love our stone chambers, such as the one we encountered at Cranberry Lake (see that chapter), and we'll learn more about them at another time while searching around during the Mead Farm hike. Older editions of the *Walk Book* used to pinpoint the chamber, identified as a root cellar, by the two planted spruce trees that flanked it but the trees came down some years ago and now identification of the site is very tough if you haven't visited it before. Let's try!

Passing through an opening in the stone wall by the boulder, bear to the right and follow the obvious path, soon passing a stone-cir-cled opening in the ground on the left. That's the rear chimney of the chamber. Continuing ahead, look for the natural spot where the brush opens up and we can turn leftward, following the topography around until the chamber presents itself (18 T 0577245, 4566161).

This chamber has obviously, to us veteran chamber hunters, been altered over the years. The cementing at the front is "new," and the chimney opening in the rear might be as well. Most notable is the sharply corbelled (interior peaked) roof (in contrast, the Mead chambers have flat slab roofs) and a wide ledge in the rear. Most of the other chambers that I know of are on the other side of the Hudson River.

After finishing our chamber inspection and continuing in the same direction as before, in a short time we'll come to a small trailside cemetery. On the other side of a low stone wall rests Civil War veteran Timothy Youmans of Company K, 56th Regiment of New York, killed in action two days before the war ended on April 9, 1865. Fresh flowers and American flags can usually be seen here, a poignant reminder that many displaced families from the pre-Park days still remember their ancestors. This is a good spot to pause for a few moments while we enjoy the silence and reflect on his sacrifice.

Beech Trail cemetery

Hiking along blue to Route 106 brings us to the end of Loop A. From here, follow 106 to the left (southerly) and then left again, bearing toward the parking lots of Lake Welch (look for another cemetery on a bluff about halfway down, looking over the lake), and you'll be back at your car promptly.

Loop B'ers, we're going to try a shortcut here. We could continue down the Beech to the Long Path, but finding the Barnes Mine is much easier from the road. We'll reluctantly take 106 southerly and climb up to Lake Welch Drive, which is closed in winter, and then turn right (west). At not-quite half a mile past Route 106, at a point where a guard rail on the left ends by a deer crossing sign, a faint footpath in the grass heads toward the mountains while passing a hillside-set stone wall that is a few yards from the road. We'll pick up that track later, but for now we'll continue on and look for the Barnes Mine.

The colonial-era Barnes Mine is about 0.1 mile east of that point, up the hill on our right (north of the road). The tailings pile is easily identified from the road, as is a short stone wall that leads

"The Pit" at Barnes Mine

uphill from LWD to the mine. Forget about finding the overgrown, neglected mine road; just bushwhack up from Lake Welch Drive once you find the mine dump. The Barnes is two long intersected cuts into the hillside; some scattered test digs and, according to *Iron Mine Trails,* the remains of what might be a powder storage shed lie 250 feet northeast of the mine.

Back on Lake Welch Drive, quiet and a bit eerie in winter, we'll now turn around and head back to that path we located earlier. It bears southerly and gently uphill to Johnsontown Road while passing by the remains of a penned area on the left as we go. Hitting blacktop and then turning right, west, we can follow the quiet country road and before long explore the grounds of Saint John's in the Wilderness Church, still in use and not actually part of the park. Just before the church, a few steps before approaching the parking lot on the right and a small cottage on the left, we'll find an unmarked path that heads off into the woods and eventually intersects with the Long Path and its turquoise blazes.

Different topography here, going from relatively short hills and level walking to some respectable mountain climbing. The hike up to the summit of Big Hill, at around 1,220 feet, is steep but short, and once at the intersection of the yellow Suffern–Bear Mountain Trail (yes, we were on a different section following Loop A) a short side trip to the right (southwesterly) will take us to the 1927 Big Hill Shelter, which offers dramatic high views of the Hudson River eastward in front of us and Manhattan's spires off in the distance downriver. This is a natural spot for a short break or lunch, as we look off in the distance at the radio towers, trying to see if we can spot the fire tower. Campers can legally sleep in this or any of the high-up park shelters overnight or pitch a tent in the vicinity at no charge. There is no outhouse or water source at any of them, but if you haven't done it, I suggest you do at some point. Harriman State Park gets well over a million visitors a year, and even the shelters can get busy on many nights, year-round.

Roller-coaster ups and downs of the trail give tantalizing glimpses of, and eventually will take us to, the 1928 Jackie Jones Mountain fire tower at 1,276 feet, the last standing fire tower in the park (not counting the scenic stone Perkins Tower on Bear Mountain). We can grip the cold metal railing and climb the shaky steps as we see if our intestinal fortitude is enough to get us to the top. The tower is unmanned, and the trap door into the cabin is locked . . . and getting up there is very scary. A sizable radio tower and support structure complex are just down the trail, and the paved road that leads to it from Route 106 can be a quick exit on a paved path.

What we do want to see are ruins, of course, and possibly the finest representation of such in the park is the old Orak site, sitting high up on the other side of Jackie Jones Mountain. The Buchanan family owned the Corn Products Refining Company, makers of Karo syrup (still on your supermarket shelves; everyone knows that Orak is Karo spelled backward). They built their grand hilltop mansion in 1923 and sold it to the park in '47, but the usual combination of time, the elements, and vandalism caused it to be razed in 1973.

Coming down the yellow trail we'll discover, without half trying, extensive remains of the site as we descend: the stone wall and its arch, dressed in ivy across the field on the right, and we see that

Abandoned utility building at Orak

Orak's decaying guardhouse

there are more explorable foundations just below. When the main path's short but steep downhill jog ends near the lower set of foundations, a faint path heads left (northwesterly) a few yards to a set of what appear to be utility buildings. One is an open shell, and the other a wood shack.

Tracing back to the yellow, our point of reference will be the ever-decaying stone guardhouse is in front of us, its moldering wood roof disappearing more and more every year. A wide driveway and some foundations are here as well.

The twisted metal remains of the estate's greenhouse is (eastward) behind the lower set of ruins. Wood and rusting metal frame contrast with and complement the wall ruins so well that we have no choice but to see all angles. We are amply rewarded, photographically speaking, for our effort, but the big-and-thorny, invasive Japanese barberry plants are taking over the area and can make exploring a potentially painful endeavor.

Once the initial inspection of Orak is completed, we really do have to pause for a moment while exploring the site. According to

Greenhouse at Orak

Trail Conference sources, the mansion's dining room was said to be able to replicate the rocking motion of a ship at sea. We have to circle the place a few times, making sure not to miss any relics or photo opportunities.

There's much to discover and photograph at Orak, and every season offers a different perspective: winter accentuates the frigid, forlorn loneliness; spring and summer's flora obscures some of the site's features but offers verdant contrast to all the rusted metal and the gray stone walls and foundations. This is a lovely spot to explore any time of the year and is a fine end to this adventure: stepping down the trail brings us right to our car, but after a rest and review of our shots, we're certainly planning to come back and explore it some more.

13
ISLAND POND RANGER CABIN

WHERE: At the end of unmarked Island Pond Road in Harriman State Park, NY

WHY: Ruins of a ranger cabin on a lake, two mines, plus a historic park shelter

DIFFICULTY: Easy; about 5 miles round-trip, with one short but steep climb

MAP: New York–New Jersey Trail Conference Map, Harriman/Bear Mountain Trails

DIRECTIONS: Palisades Parkway north to exit 14. Make a right onto Route 98, which becomes Route 106. We begin at the parking area on Route 106, about 1.5 miles west of the intersection of Route 106 and Seven Lakes Drive. There are a few parking pullouts in the vicinity, but the one we want has the White Bar Trail (white-blazed) crossing the road nearby.

This is a good hike for beginners or families with young children because the terrain has minimal elevation changes, except for the path up to the shelter. The features we're looking for are close to each other and visually impressive.

We'll start out by picking up the White Bar Trail and following it north. The WB and unmarked Island Pond Road will soon join together for a short time. The WB bears right after a few minutes of walking, but we will stay to the left on unblazed Island Pond Road.

This is a wild, attractive part of the park, and this section makes for pleasant, mostly level hiking except for the rise on the way up to

the shelter later on. At 0.75 mile from the car, turn right (east) on the yellow-blazed Dunning Trail. In a few yards you will encounter the dark Boston Mine, a cut in the hillside to the left of the trail. Walk through the cut ahead of you and look around to see the actual mine shaft, now flooded. It was thought to have been active around 1880, mining magnetite iron. This is a fine mine site and a good warm-up for the ranger cabin ruin.

Once you are back on Island Pond Road, continue heading north, straight past the Arden-Surebridge Trail (red-blazed) to the ruin of the ranger cabin. The Garfield Mine lurks off a left-handed spur trail just before you reach the old parking area for the cabin. The Garfield is a series of uninteresting Parrott Brothers exploratory trenches (see the "Mines! All Mines!" chapter for more on them) from around 1880, usually filled with water and a bit tricky to identify as a mine.

The cabin ruin sits at the south tip of scenic Island Pond and was built as a place for park rangers to party and entertain sometime around the 1920s. In 1963, idiotic vandals playing with matches destroyed it. The stone foundation, the chimney, and some walls

Boston Mine

Ranger cabin walls

Ranger cabin chimney

are all that's left. It is an entertaining task trying to picture what the cabin looked like, but clearly it was an attractive building in an exceptionally picturesque setting.

This will be our lunch spot. After lunch, suit up and we'll retrace our steps on Island Pond Road (south) back to the yellow Dunning Trail. Left turn onto Dunning (east) and follow it up and down through the woods, passing the Boston Mine and the White Bar Trail (they run together for 0.15 mile), eventually reaching the red-on-white-blazed Ramapo-Dunderburg Trail.

Follow the R-D to the right (south) as it climbs up a rocky ridge and peaks out at 1,382 feet. Traveling south, at 0.2 mile from the intersection you will soon encounter the Bald Rock Shelter, built in 1933 with stone taken from the immediate area. Backpackers can hike to these shelters and stay overnight, first come, first served. The shelters are open in the front and do little to protect you against bugs, critters, or serious weather. Personally, I'd rather sleep in a tent at night.

There is a network of these shelters scattered throughout the park, usually taking advantage of high viewpoints. The Civilian

Conservation Corps built them mostly during the 1920s and 1930s. In fact, to digress a moment, Harriman State Park itself owes much to Roosevelt's New Deal. The roads through the park, landscaping, construction of shelters and buildings, damming of lakes, and place names all stem from this period.

These shelters make excellent day hike destinations in their own right. Some have fireplaces that are suitable for cooking. (Tip: Gather up some firewood or bring match-light charcoal and burn a burger up there.) People leave all sorts of things in these shelters such as books, cans of food, and sometimes cooking grills.

Continuing south on the R-D, bear right when you reach the Nurian Trail (white), at 0.75 mile south of the shelter. Once you reach the White Bar Trail at about 0.4 mile, turn left (south), and follow it back to the parking area. Quite a lovely little loop we just did!

14
MINES! ALL MINES!

WHERE: Harriman State Park, NY

WHY: Multiple old iron mines, historic shelter, forest fire site, Times Square of the woods

DIFFICULTY: Challenging; 8 miles, with significant elevation changes

MAP: New York–New Jersey Trail Conference Map, Northern Harriman trails

UTM COORDINATES: Hogencamp Mine: 18 T 0573780, 4566182
Pine Swamp Mine: 18 T 0574269, 4566805
Pine Swamp Mine eyebolt: 18 T 0574296, 4566878

DIRECTIONS: New York State Thruway (I-87) to exit 15A, Route 17 north. Take 17 north to Seven Lakes Drive, and turn right, into the park. Take Seven Lakes Drive toward Bear Mountain, and park at the lot on Lake Skannatiti, 0.7 mile north of the Kanawauke Circle.

Harriman State Park is truly a great destination for us ruin-hunters. Iron mines, historic shelters, old cemeteries, and more await our explorations in just about all the different areas of this park. Unmarked woods roads, arteries to long-vanished farms and mines, lace the park. Besides all that, it is a very attractive park with many different variations in landscape as you hike from one section to the next. On this tour we will check out a few iron mines and also Times Square, a well-known trail junction where several paths intersect. When hiking in this section, you can't help but cross it at least once. You should bring the Big Flashlight on this trip.

After locking the car, locate the red-triangle-blazed Arden-Sure-bridge Trail, and follow it westerly and uphill, leaving behind the citizens who hang around the lake, as we climb up to Pine Swamp Mountain. After hiking for a short time, our first reward is a fine 1,125-foot viewpoint overlooking the lake with clear views to the southwest. The A-SB undulates up and down for another 0.45 mile and soon gets interesting.

Passing through the second of two low-lying hemlock groves that we'll encounter, it's time to start looking down. At the end of the hemlocks the trail goes up and doglegs to the left as we pick up the old mine road (still the Arden-Surebridge Trail). Just before the left turn are some noteworthy glacial erratics, but what we came to see is some iron ore. It's scattered all around us in great rusted quantities. Whip out your magnetometer (or a compass if you only have that) and start reading some rocks. Some of their iron content is magnetic and will have an effect on a compass needle.

I've frequently impressed the ladies by picking up iron ore chunks and breaking off nice big pieces (with an appropriate accompanying grunt), easily accomplished owing to the oxidation of the iron (but they sure didn't know *that!*). Iron ore is normally a slate gray but becomes red-streaked and flaky as it rusts, so follow the trail of rusted iron up to the road and start looking around.

Mine pits are scattered around the trail, and there is an impressive horizontal cut on the right side of the trail just before we approach a wide stream. Let's cross over and then pick up the yellow-blazed Dunning Trail, heading left (southwesterly). Pine Swamp is now clearly presented on our left. Follow Dunning down a short distance to where we see a cleft (usually with a stream running through, passing under the trail in a culvert) in the hillside on our right. If we begin to follow the stream uphill, before we get very far we can see a mine cut on the left (south) side of the stream. It's a warm-up for things to come.

To find the Pine Swamp Mine, continue along the yellow Dunning (which also passed the Boston Mine in another hike) for about 60 yards until we see a faint trail by a yellow-blazed tree. It leads sharply uphill past familiar black tailings to a clearing, with the main mine opening just a few feet in (18 T 0574269, 4566805).

Pine Swamp Mine

The Pine Swamp Mine is exciting. A Parrott Brothers acquisition, this mine was worked from 1830 off and on until 1880. The shaft runs over 100 feet along a diagonal vein, and the walls of the tunnel are about 40 feet high in some places. I've heard it compared to a subway tunnel. There is an opening in the roof at the far end where sunlight comes through on a clear day, emphasizing the sheer volume of the excavation. While it is very tempting to step inside and walk from

Eyebolt in rock

one end to the other, be advised that signs on the site declare it off limits. The ore vein that was being mined continues below the mine entrance into an area that is now flooded. After exploring the mine area, exit back out to the level area just outside the mine. Head to the left (north), following the remains of old roads that circled through. They lead to other cuts and shafts of the mine, and an odd iron eyelet protruding from the top of a boulder.

Robert and Peter Parrott owned iron mines and foundries in the area and needed all the ore they could get their hands on. In the world of munitions, two of the nineteenth century's greatest innovations were the rifled bore and banded cannon barrel. The rifled bore shot ordnance out with a spin (think of a football in flight), improving distance and accuracy. The banded cannon barrel was wrapped with external iron bands. The bands increased the strength of the cannon by preventing ruptures upon firing, and it also allowed quicker breech (rear) loading. The Parrott brothers didn't invent these methods but were able to develop reliable manufacturing processes, especially the secure placing of the iron bands. Foundries owned by the Parrotts produced many different cast iron finished goods, but weapons were foremost. The West Point Foundry area that we will hike in another chapter was a major Parrott operation and the site where the banding process was developed.

Once we're done exploring the mine area, return to the yellow Dunning Trail. The Dunning is a wide, mostly level woods road at this point as we skirt the swamp and head south. When we go by the Long Path (turquoise blue–blazed), continue straight ahead for a few yards and then look around. This is the site of the 1870–1885

Hogencamp Mine (18 T 0573780, 4566182 puts us in the middle of the complex); a series of open trench cuts are visible on the right side (west) of the trail. There are six mine trenches to discover, some foundations, cuts, pits, and an impressive opening into the hillside. It doesn't have one spectacular shaft such as the Pine Swamp Mine, but pound-for-pound has possibly the greatest concentration of relics of any mine site in this park. Various sources note the site of a village along the Long Path, northwest of the Dunning junction and above the mine site.

Follow the tailings piles, and all will be revealed. Most notable is the high, deep-slotted mine cut that appears to tunnel under the Long Path as that trail heads up and over the mine site on its way to Times Square. A piece of rebar sticking up out of the rock (part of a safety barrier, one would think) identifies the cut from the Long Path.

Continuing along on the Dunning, the forest changes from swamp to drier ground as the elevation rises. Trees give way to large, open expanses of rock faces and domes. As we approach the red Ramapo-Dunderburg Trail, it becomes apparent that there was a forest fire here. In fact, sometime during the mid-1980s, a fire came through here, damaging many acres. It remains interesting to see how the recovery process continues. Baby pines are everywhere, as are bleached and burnt trunks of probably second-growth pine.

Warning: The intersection of the yellow Dunning and red Ramapo-Dunderburg is easy to miss. Be attentive and read your topo carefully.

With Hogencamp Mountain looming on our right (easterly), pick up the R-D and take it to the right, northeasterly. This is a very primal looking part of the park; burnt forest, rocks, and boulders of all sizes strewn around and few healthy mature trees. Sharp white pine trunks killed in the fire of the mid '80s cover the hillsides as far as we can see, spiking skyward. Just think back to what the Pine Swamp area looked like. We'll do some climbing up large open rock faces as we make our way up to Ship Rock, supposedly so named because it resembles (to some trailblazers) the upended hull of a ship. Okay, if they say so. To me it looks like a big stone hill. On a hot summer day, the reflected heat from the bare rocks can be intense.

More rock hopping will eventually lead us down to the famous trail junction known as Times Square.

A stone fireplace marks Times Square, as does a large glacial erratic boulder, emblazoned with the various trail names and "arrowed" to point the way. Three different blazed trails meet here, and to the north is the unmarked Surebridge Mine Road. The Long Path (LP) and Arden-Surebridge (A-SB) trails meet the Ramapo-Dunderburg (R-D) Trail at this point. Go left (north) on the LP/A-SB trails, and shortly they both bend to the left. A wide woods road is now before us: the Surebridge Mine Road.

We have an easy, mostly level half-mile or so on Surebridge Mine Road until we approach our next iron mine. The Surebridge Mine appears on our right just before an intersection with the Bottle Cap Trail (blazed with white bottle caps).

This 1880 mine produced some 458 tons of iron ore for the Parrott Brothers, the mine owners. The Surebridge Mine has the unmistakable feeling of industrial activity in years past. The site is generally a series of cuts, trenches, pits, rock piles, and flooded shafts that scar the landscape endlessly, some features being revealed by a little off-trail poking around. It is interesting to explore this area with or without other references. There are no enterable shafts (or adits) at this mine.

Greenwood Mine

Continuing down the mine road for another half-mile, our last iron mine of the day is on our right, just before the old road meets the Appalachian Trail. The 1838-era Greenwood Mine is yet another Parrott iron mine, with ore shipping to the various Parrott holdings. There is a 100-foot flooded trench just beside the road. Tailings piles, flooded pits, and variously shaped cuts are all within easy exploration radius. By keeping our eyes open we can locate the road that leads uphill to the main mine shaft, which is also flooded.

Our next move is to take the Appalachian Trail to the right (east) up Fingerboard Mountain to the shelter there (notice we join with the R-D Trail along the way). The Fingerboard Shelter (1928) sits at 1,300 feet, with Lake Tioratti below us and to the east. This is a comfortable spot to eat lunch or just take a break.

Leaving the AT, we'll take the R-D south (we took it north earlier today) down Fingerboard Mountain and back to Times Square. Pick up the turquoise blue–blazed Long Path (which runs from the George Washington Bridge to Whiteface Mountain in the Adirondacks) and follow it to the left (south) over Pine Swamp Mountain and back to the car. Although we explored a good number of interesting Harriman mines on this little excursion, our appetite for old iron has only been whetted for future adventures.

15
MOUNT HOPE HISTORICAL PARK

WHERE: Mount Hope, NJ

WHY: Extensive mining artifacts and ruins

DIFFICULTY: Easy; 3 to 4 miles, with minor elevation changes

MAP: Mount Hope Historical Park map, Morris County Parks Commission

DIRECTIONS: I-80 west to exit 35, Mount Hope Avenue. After 0.5 mile, turn left onto Richard Mine Road, and then turn right after 0.7 mile onto Coburn Road (turns into Teabo Road). The park entrance is on our left 0.7 mile from the turn. The way to the park is well signed from the interstate exit.

This small park has the greatest concentration of ruins and mine pits in this book. Although the hiking is actually minimal, budget a good three-and-a-half hours or so for proper exploration. There are many side trails that are hard to ignore.

After parking, locate the kiosk with maps at the eastern end of the lot, and read the historical information posted on the board. According to the board information, mining started at the Mount Hope sites about 1772 and continued until 1958. The largest workings were known as the Richard, Teabo, and Allen Mines. These three different veins of magnetite iron ore were mined on this site, with the earliest known commercial mining occurring around 1820. Rockaway Township mines produced about 50 percent of all of New Jersey's iron during the eighteenth century.

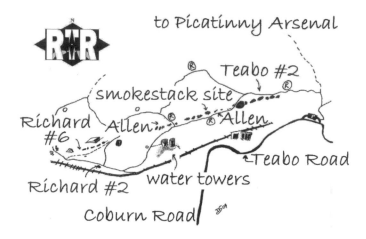

Let's follow the trail up from the lot to a point where it splits into a red-blazed trail bearing left, and white- and blue-blazed trails bearing to the right. More on the white and blue trails later on. We'll take the red trail up the hill.

After about fifteen minutes of walking from the parking lot, the trail turns sharply left at a sign that warns:

NO HIKING
FEDERAL GOVERNMENT PROPERTY
TURN AROUND TO CONTINUE HIKING

If we ignore the sign and continue straight, we'll come up on the grounds of the Picatinny Arsenal, where Uncle Sam devises advanced weapons for the military. Not a good place to sneak up on! Besides, we've noticed that the diggings and pits have begun, so let's respect the warning on the sign and continue with the red trail.

The mine pits are now coming fast and furious as we hike on. We soon see a post with a number "4" on it, which corresponds to a historical narrative on the back of the map. This would be Teabo #2, worked from 1880 to 1883. The Teabo Mine was one of the three major mines on this property.

Continuing on the trail, we'll soon come to a split where red branches off red. Stay to the left and post #5 comes up, the Allen

Mine site, named for Jabez Allen, who was the property owner between 1848 and 1868. Numerous trenches and pits litter the area, following the Richard ore vein. The Allen Tunnel and smoke stack sites are just ahead at marker #6. In 1855, the tunnel ran 600 feet from Teabo Road (outside the park) into the ore body and was the main access into the Allen Mine. No visible remains of either the tunnel or the stack are extant here.

Yes, there sure are plenty of holes in the ground around here. We're both hoping things get a bit more interesting, right?

In a short time we come to another trail split, this time an orange trail branching off from red. Bear right onto the red trail, and then, left in a short time onto the other end of the orange trail (red heads off to the right). There are a few trenches and pits along the trail in this section and a few mysterious vent pipes poking out of the ground. What are they venting? How do we get to it?

Soon enough, after hiking for about twenty minutes or so, the trail passes unmarked spurs that veer off into points unknown. One heads toward a group of houses. A broken brick pillar becomes visible on the right-hand side of the trail, a sign that some good discoveries are coming up soon. Point #7, the Richard Mine and Richard 6, an 1897 shaft, soon present themselves. Both operations worked parts of the Richard vein. Right around this post we will see a concrete trapezoidal structure up the hill on your left. We will now begin our explorations in earnest.

As we bushwhack up to the trapezoid and look around, several mine structures will come into view. There is a concrete platform nearby with iron rods at the far end. Steel cables lie about and a bent water pipe is just behind it. Near the ground there is an iron ring set into the vertical far corner of the concrete pad. Several coils of steel cables are here, too. We can see the open corner remains of a building across the way. Climb up a bit and a faint trail becomes visible. It is indicated as a dotted line on the park map, and it is not the bold dotted line at post #8. Keep climbing. Deep trenches are on our left, as well as more coils of steel cable. Someone was hoisting a large amount of heavy rock here.

Right at the spot where two cable coils sit, the "heavy dotted line" path joins in from the right. We'll take that a little later. For

Coils of cables

now, follow the road uphill to where we see a fenced area come up on the right. Remains of the hoist platform are seen, and there is another concrete platform across the path from it.

Peer through the fence for the most impressive sight yet, the deep dig of the (Richard?) mineshaft. An enormous steel pipe sticks straight up through the dig, capped with a huge concrete block. There is also the opportunity for some archeological garbage exploration, as this must have been the town dumping area at some point. Old appliances rust in the trenches surrounding the mine. It is true that this hike is not exactly a "back to nature" experience. Let's hike up to the end of the road and then turn around and head back toward the orange trail. Once at the orange trail, do not continue to the left (east) but backtrack west a bit. Some stone foundations are on the north side of the trail and worth a peek. Now we can head east, passing point #8, and the Richard 2 shaft. This was the site of the mine's primary shaft, where ore was hoisted out by bucket. In 1884, a cart system was installed to replace the buckets. By 1886, close to 72,000 tons of iron ore was extracted. The mine was abandoned in 1903.

More vaguely recognizable ruins dot the area as we head toward post #9, site of the Mount Hope Mineral Railroad right of way.

Examining a foundation

We've noticed the large number of railroad ties on this part of the trail. At the point where the orange trail veers to the left, a road appears straight before us and seems to be the logical extension of the trail. We'll leave the trail and go straight on the old rail bed for a little while. An impressive building ruin lies at the end, badly damaged and covered in graffiti. In fact, there is a great deal to see around here: railroad ties, foundations, remains of platforms and supports, and probably more hidden in the undergrowth.

Explore carefully and then look on the hillside above for the two water tanks perched there. A road leads up toward them. We'll take it, and our friend the orange trail reveals itself quite soon. Back on orange, climbing up the hillside under the power lines, we can get to the tanks easily via a spur trail that is impossible to miss. At this point, we actually have some decent views to the south toward Mount Hope.

Continuing on the orange, we come to site #10: Turner's Whim Shaft, Trenton Iron Company's Shaft, Old Shafts 1 and 2, Whim Shaft 1, and Old Shaft 1. The earliest mine workings in the park occurred at this site, probably around 1830. The Richard vein was worked via the shallow pits seen here. Continue on to the junction of the red and orange trails that we passed earlier. For the sake of completeness, we'll bear left (north) on red and follow red (passing the orange trail we followed earlier) straight back to the parking lot, making this trail a lazy figure eight through the old mine workings.

Abandoned building at Mount Hope Historical Park

16
OVERLOOK MOUNTAIN HOUSE

WHERE: On top of Overlook Mountain near Woodstock, NY

WHY: Massive concrete ruins of a hotel, high viewpoint, fire tower

DIFFICULTY: Moderate; about 5 miles round-trip, all uphill to the ruin

MAP: New York–New Jersey Trail Conference Map, Northern Catskill Trails

DIRECTIONS: New York State Thruway (I-87) north to exit 19. Go west toward Pinehill on Route 28 for about 7 miles to Route 375. Make a right turn on 375 (north) toward Woodstock. Follow 375 to where it ends at Route 212, and turn left. From Route 212, head into the town center at Woodstock, and make a right turn (north) on Ulster County Route 33. (The junction may not be signed. Look for a public parking sign at the turn.) Ulster 33 will eventually turn right about a mile after the junction with Route 212, but stay straight and follow the road (Meads Mountain Road) to the signed Overlook Parking Area on your right.

There are few remains of the once magnificent cluster of huge mountain retreats that graced the Catskill Mountains region in the early part of the 1900s. Together we will hike to the best-preserved example of this group.

From the parking lot, follow the Overlook Spur Trail (red-blazed) 2.5 miles to the top. You can't get lost on this trail. It's pretty straightforward and climbs up to the summit on the old carriage road that served the hotel.

Well, not really *this* hotel exactly. The first Overlook House was built in 1871 and destroyed by fire in 1875. The second Catskill

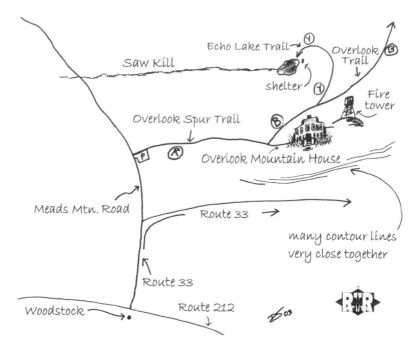

Mountain House on the site was built in 1878, and it also fell to fire in 1924. That structure was three stories high and anchored to the mountain via steel cables. Finally, someone had the idea to make the third out of fireproof poured concrete. The stock market crash of 1929 stopped work sometime around 1933, and what remains on top of the mountain is the never-completed concrete shell of the third Overlook Mountain House and some other buildings.

Other massive Catskill Mountain hotels followed soon after the first hotel was successful, peaking in 1881 with the thousand-room-plus Hotel Kaaterskill at North Lake. Sadly, all have vanished, mainly lost to fires. A circular day hike around the North/South Lake State Park area will bring you to the sites of two of these hotels, although nothing but a clearing remains of either of them (and therefore, that particular hike is not mentioned in this book).

The Overlook Spur Trail tops out by the hotel ruin at about 3,100 feet. Most of the hotel is easily accessible to our nosing around, but some deep drops and overgrowth prohibit entry into other areas. Odd artifacts abound, including toilets, bathtubs, window frames, and fixtures. There are nonstop photo opportunities here. In addition to the main building, there is a smaller hotel structure behind the big ruin.

After poking around, head over to the recently restored fire tower (sitting at 3,140 feet). This 60-foot tower has been here since 1950 and is one of five original remaining Catskill fire towers. Interestingly, parts of it are from an older 1927 tower that stood on Gallis Hill, near Kingston. After a nerve-testing climb up the tower to the 7-foot square cabin on top, we can see the Berkshire Hills in Massachusetts over to the east, the regal Hudson River in front of them, and the Taconic Mountains in New York. The Ashokan Reservoir and the Shawangunk Mountains are on our side of the river to the south. Our lunch spot is at the picnic table down below.

Walking to the east of the fire tower brings us to a high ledge with about 2,000 feet of air below us. Carved into this ledge are names and dates from over a hundred years ago, if you believe all of them. Let's face it, anyone can carve "David 1802" into stone and make it seem authentic. There's no way to tell what is real and what is a hoax,

Overlook Hotel in spring

although I do believe most of them are actually historic graffiti. Some of the carvings took some time to do and are impressively skillful.

We'll take our time enjoying the view and the ruins, then it's back down the Overlook Spur Trail to our car. Maybe we'll do some dinner and faux-hippie gawking in Woodstock before we drive home.

Hotel lobby

The view from an upper level

17
THE PERGOLA

WHERE: Palisades Interstate Park, NJ, beginning at the State Line Lookout

WHY: Abandoned sections of old Route 9W, Peanut Leap (or Half Moon) Falls, remains of the fanciful Italian Garden, Giant Stairs, Women's Federation Monument, Timken Estate remains

DIFFICULTY: Moderate; about 6 miles round-trip, with some steep ascents and descents

MAP: New York–New Jersey Trail Conference Map: Hudson Palisades Trails, NJ section

WEBSITE: www.njpalisades.org

DIRECTIONS: Palisades Interstate Parkway northbound to the State Line Lookout parking area near exit 3.

Relatively new discoveries await us as we begin our explorations into the Hudson Palisades.

If you are like me, you likely pass the Palisades on your way up to other parks, such as Harriman. I've always known that there were interesting ruins and historic sites in this region, but it wasn't until I started researching this book that I discovered exactly what the story is here. In this chapter, we will encounter ruins of sculpted gardens, an old mansion site, an obelisk state line boundary marker, a castle-like monument, and an abandoned roadbed.

There are actually a few old mansion sites and worthy ruins in Palisades Interstate Park. The problem is that much of the Long

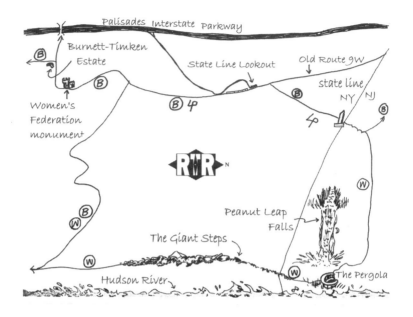

Path, which passes by the best ruins, also runs along the Palisades
Interstate Parkway. For me, this negates the nature experience
because the traffic noise is intrusive. If you're interested, the section
of the LP above and below the park headquarters has plenty of fun
remains to seek out. The park sponsors historic hikes during the
summer to many of these sites: for details see www.njpalisades.org/
calendar.html, and look for the "Millionaires Row" tour.

The Lookout Inn at the State Line Lookout area is a fine (seasonal) spot to buy a lunch "to go" for our journey, or to peruse
assorted books of historic interest. Once inside, be sure to look for
various displayed pamphlets and brochures that outline the many
ski trails and unmarked paths that lace the area. Like much of Palisades Interstate Park (which includes Harriman and Bear Mountain
State Parks), the Works Progress Administration was responsible for
constructing the inn and many of the more impressive trail "aids"
(steps, etc.) that we will encounter, and as usual, the workers did
thoroughly professional job.

After we get our gear together, let's walk over to the scenic
overlook and check out the view. Hawks circle lazily about, taking

advantage of the swirling updrafts caused by the cliffs. It's a sheer 500-foot drop down to the Hudson River, as it is in many other spots along our trail. Due caution is strongly advised. The only higher cliffs I know of are on Breakneck Ridge. Hastings-on-Hudson is directly across the river on the New York side. Yonkers is further south; Dobbs Ferry is to the north.

We begin by walking over to the northern end of the lot, near the inn. Locating the blue-blazed Long Path (which runs along the unused 1926 Route 9W for a short time), let's take it and eventually separate from old 9W as we head into the woods. There is a wooden sign at the split indicating various trail destinations. After about a half-hour of walking, a concrete New York–New Jersey state boundary marker looms ahead on the left side of the trail, placed when a modern survey laid out the definitive border, which had been in dispute since colonial times. The fence behind it marks the property line between Palisades Interstate Park and the Lamont-Doherty Earth Observatory. The trail runs through its property for a short time. Follow the LP as it attends the fence for a short time and then passes through a gate into New York State. The trail runs northerly across sheer cliff tops with a steel cabled fence preventing unfortunate 500-foot mistakes.

The Tappan Zee Bridge in New York State is now visible ahead of us, running from Tarrytown on the east shore to Nyack on the west. The bridge name comes from the Tappan Indian tribe of the area, and *zee,* Dutch for "sea." When I was in Holland some years ago, I asked a tour guide for some translations of New York place names. He told me that Tappan Zee translates roughly to "pouring sea," as *tappan* means "pour" in Dutch. Think of a beer tap. But officially, it's the Indian reference that gets the credit. Below the Tap on the left (west side) is the town of Piermont, with its famous artificial land pier running a mile into the Hudson, and below that sits the largest saltwater marsh on the river.

Most of the hiking consists of rock-hopping as we quickly descend toward the river. After about an hour of hiking (and about fifteen or so minutes of walking past the gate), the LP drops steeply downhill on endless WPA steps. The river seems to be getting closer up to now, but at this point, the trail veers sharply to the left (west), crosses two wooden footbridges, and then meets up with the northern terminus of the white-blazed Shore Trail. The following wooden sign is posted at the intersection:

SHORE TRAIL
WARNING: HIKING VERY DIFFICULT NEXT TWO MILES

Is that amusing or ominous? Either way, the white Shore Trail descends eastward rapidly, bordering a cascade on the right and streams coming in from the left (in wet weather). Wooden boards secured tightly across the path aid the hapless hiker on the steepest sections. The trail can get muddy and slippery. I know: I slipped on the slick mud and tumbled downhill a few yards, scratched up the length of my right arm, and smacked my leg against a rock, bruising it from hip to knee. I hobbled painfully down the trail past the Peanut Leap waterfall (sometimes known as Half Moon Falls, in honor of Henry Hudson's ship) to the safe haven of the offbeat Italian Gardens ruin at the base of the falls.

Mary Lawrence Tonnetti has forever cemented her name in park lore as the mind behind the Italian Garden. At the turn of the

Peanut Leap Falls

Steps near the Pergola

century, she was a well-known artist (and early 1900s–era hippie) from a wealthy family. After traveling in Italy, she became enamored with the architecture, and once she returned home, formed a family owned property at the base of the falls into her own eccentric party spot. She built platforms, staircases, heavy stone walls, arched alcoves, and reflecting pools with lion head fountains at this location. She entertained her New York art crowd friends with exotic parties, spaghetti dinners, and various other artful events at the site. The most famous spot was "The Pergola," a small colonnaded sitting area right on the shore of the Hudson River. Above the columns was a semicircular concrete rail draped with grape vines. All in all, the garden was a fanciful spot that was a favorite of travelers, and still is.

As is the case so often, time, the elements, and vandals have leveled the place to the reduced condition it is in now. The steps are broken. The Pergola columns are in pieces along the ground, visible only if you go looking for them. The reflecting pools are filled in with debris and barely recognizable. The falls remain strong, though, and you can still sit quietly on the Pergola benches and reflect on the river. With some imagination, we can still fabricate what must have been here, and possibly even hear the echoes of those long-gone avant-garde parties. We will undoubtedly have company as we rest here, as other hikers come by to investigate the garden. This is one of the most popular hiking destinations in the park, and I'm certain Mary would like that.

The Italian Garden

The white Shore Trail heads southward, following the mighty Hudson River as it brings us through the Giant Steps section of the trail. The steps aren't especially giant, but there are many of them, sometimes comically so. It's slow going crossing the Giant Steps because it's all high impact pounding to your ankles and knees for two miles.

Finally, the blue/white trail appears, and we begin the arduous ascent to the top of the cliffs. Slow and steady is the way to do it; never sit down and rest only briefly as you trudge up the 500 feet from river to Long Path.

Once we meet the Long Path, bear left (south) and take it 0.2 mile to the Women's Federation Watchtower, a monument to the organization that began founding the Palisades Interstate Park in the early part of the twentieth century to protect the cliffs from the increasing amount of blasting that was going on at the time. The rock that was being removed from the cliffs was used for Manhattan skyscrapers and ships' ballast. We can climb up the short staircase to the top level and take in the river view that the Federation worked so hard to preserve. Just down the trail (to the south) is the site of the Burnett (Timken) Estate, one of the many "mansion" sites that the Long Path features as it makes its way through the palisades.

Artist Cora Timken and scientist John Burnett did experiments with magnetism in their copper-domed lab on this site. The only identifiable remains are of the pool just off the LP, a few yards south of the Women's Federation monument, near an intersection with a dirt road. The lab was destroyed by fire in 1939, and if that weren't bad enough, Cora's artwork was stored inside. Somewhere out of sight is their bomb shelter. It's underneath us somewhere, 100 feet long and hand-carved out of the rock.

During construction of the Palisades Interstate Parkway, the plans called for the road to go right through the Burnett property. A year after Cora's death, the family was awarded $1.5 million for the plot. The state razed parts of the estate but never did completely demolish it. We'll return to our vehicles by traveling northward on the blue-blazed Long Path, enjoying one of the few sections of the trail that is removed from the ever-present parkway.

18
RAMAPO VALLEY COUNTY RESERVATION

WHERE: Near Mahwah, NJ

WHY: Mill ruin, high views, two old iron mines, two house ruins, active scout camp, even out of season

DIFFICULTY: Challenging; 9 miles, with significant elevation changes

MAP: New York–New Jersey Trail Conference Map, North Jersey Trails

UTM COORDINATES: Nickel Mine 1: 18 T 0566932, 4549332
Nickel Mine 2: 18 T 0566919, 4549354

DIRECTIONS: New York State Thruway (I-87) north to exit 15, Route 287 south/Route 17 south. Once on the ramp, bear left immediately and exit at Route 17 south. Take 17 south to Route 202 (Ramapo Valley Road) and bear left at the end of the ramp toward Ramapo College. Begin at the Ramapo State Forest parking area, about 2 miles west of Route 17 in Mahwah, NJ.

Many smaller attractions add up to an outstanding day in the woods on this hike in northern New Jersey. For best results, do this particular hike in the fall or winter, when the scout camp will most likely be empty. Be advised that the trail map distributed by the park is inaccurate and should not be trusted. Our route will bring us up to the Nickel Mine and, crossing into Ringwood State Park, the Butler Mine and some viewpoints. The Boy Scout camp and some ruins round out the day.

As with most ore-bearing regions, this one, too, had mines, sawmills, and foundries. It was also logged to the ground, probably

more than once. The Hopkins and Dickinson Manufacturing Company in Darlington processed much of the ore that was mined here.
A. B. Darling, of Darlington fame, eventually bought the property
and turned it into his estate.

Right away, we notice the mill ruin on the river. We'll pick up
the first trail by crossing the bridge into the park and continuing
straight on the Silver Trail past Scarlet Oak Pond. The blue-blazed
Ridge Trail comes in shortly. Let us begin our ascent up to the
Nickel Mine. The hiking trails in this part of the park are mostly on
woods roads.

At 1.1 miles past the parking lot, the Havemeyer Trail (blue-
white-blazed) terminates at the Ridge Trail. Distances in this park
are deceiving. It doesn't look that long on the map, but it's taken

Noah explores the old mill

almost an hour just to get to this point. Once we're at the junction of the Havemeyer and Ridge Trails, face south, looking back the way we came along the Ridge Trail. The Havemeyer Trail is now on our left.

Point to the two o'clock position on the horizon with your right hand. Heading a few hundred feet down the embankment on that bearing (southwesterly) will bring us to the Nickel Mine. There are two mine pits on a level shelf at the site. One is circular and flooded and surrounded by tailings (18 T 0566919, 4549354). A few feet to the east is a flooded trench with drainage at the west end (18 T 0566932, 4549332).

The Hopkins and Dickinson Manufacturing Company did some exploratory work in these mountains. The firm was looking for iron and nickel, but mines such as this never produced ore on any meaningful scale.

Retrace back to the blue Ridge Trail, and we'll continue to the next mine, the Butler. Follow the blue around to the Silver Trail, where we bear to the right (northwesterly) and continue to the

Nickel Mine

Red-Silver Trail, taking that to the right and up. A new orange-blazed trail appears that is not on any map that I have, so we'll just ignore it. At some point around here, we left Ramapo Valley County Reservation and entered into Ringwood State Park.

After an invigorating climb, Bear Swamp Lake is finally reached. (After almost two hours of walking, you'd think we'd have covered more ground.) Here, blazes get a bit funny. The blue-blazed Shore

Trail circles the lake and conjoins with the Cannonball Trail (blazed by a red "C").

The Cannonball Trail is a historic trail that supposedly follows old roads to unnamed mining and foundry sites where ordnance was manufactured in Revolutionary War days. As far as I know, this is all legend. The real problem here is that the Cannonball is possibly the worst marked regional trail that I've come across. It makes its way along, but the blazes in this area are of little help if indeed this is the trail you're trying to follow. It deteriorates even more over to the west in Ramapo Mountain State Forest, where we'll be looking for a mansion ruin on another day. Anyway, bear to the right (north) and try to follow the dual Cannonball/Shore Trail (blue-blazed) as it hugs the lake. This is a good spot for a short rest.

Afterward, continue around the lake on the blue Shore Trail. (What do you know, the Cannonball has been following us all along. Wouldn't know it by the blazes.) The yellow Hoeferlin Trail joins up on the opposite side of the lake. By the way, the New York–New Jersey Trail Conference map is correct in blaze designation here, so don't follow the county map. Yellow and blue blazes run concurrently for a few yards, bearing southwest, until the blue bears left and the yellow heads to the right. Take yellow and climb up to the Butler Mine.

It isn't hard to find the Butler. It runs alongside the trail 0.2 mile northeast of the Crossover Trail (white-blazed). The Butler was the site of exploration digs and activity in the middle of the 1860s through the 1880s. There are a series of pits and trenches on the site, easily found by the trail. We've worked hard to get here, so it's now officially lunchtime. Elevation at this point is about 1,100 feet. After lunch, it's back on yellow and headed in the same direction (south).

Enough with the mines right now; let's find some views. Continuing on yellow, passing the white Crossover Trail, ultimately brings us to Ilgenstein Rock, a fine lookout at about 1,100 feet. Bear Swamp Lake is below us, and on a clear day we can see Manhattan. Continue on yellow, and soon we'll get to Erskine Lookout, this time facing the west and Wanaque Reservoir. Pick up the green-blazed trail that meets the yellow-blazed trail at Erskine Lookout. Again, at this point the Trail Conference map is correct and the county map is not.

The green trail drops and unexpectedly reaches Camp Yaw Paw on Cannonball Lake, still in use as a Boy Scout camp. In the off-season it appears to be abandoned at first glance, but soon we see clearly that it is not. There are lots of buildings and lean-tos around the property to explore, most of them locked and secured.

Gathering back in camp, we have a decision to make. If time and daylight allow, we can find the yellow-blazed Hoeferlin Trail (according to the map the Cannonball is also somewhere around here) and follow it westward down to the yellow/silver trail, then eastward (left) past a ruin and back to the car. On my last visit, the trails were very poorly marked in this section, and I found it simpler to just follow the camp road down to the ruin. The other advantage to this route is that we parallel a series of cascades as we descend. A major disadvantage is that walking downhill on asphalt is hard on hiking boot–clad feet. However you get there, the twin buildings of the ruin are just off the camp road at the junction of the yellow/silver trail. What the heck were they? Inquiries at this point have proven fruitless, so your guess is as good as mine.

The yellow/silver trail to the left (east) goes up and over Matty Price Hill as it heads back to the silver trail and our car. We feel this one. Although the distance on this hike was only about 9 miles, our feet are saying "more!"

19
THE ROOMY MINE

WHERE: Norvin Green State Forest, NJ

WHY: A big iron mine that we can enter, panoramic high viewpoint along the way

DIFFICULTY: Challenging; 10 miles, with significant elevation changes and possible water crossing issues

MAP: New York–New Jersey Trail Conference Map, North Jersey Trails

UTM COORDINATES: Blue Mine: 18 T 0557366, 4545594
Roomy Mine: 18 T 0557512, 4546142

DIRECTIONS: Route 80 west to exit 53, Route 23 north. Take 23 about 10 miles to Route 511, and make a right turn toward the town of Butler. Follow 511 as it snakes through Butler. Make a left at Hamburg Turnpike (first left after Arch Street). Bear right on Glenwild Avenue as it goes uphill, and look for the yellow blazes at a pullout on the right after a mile or so. Glenwild Avenue is also called Otter Hole Road.

This investigation is unusual in that there's plenty of hiking but only two sites for us to discover, one being a flooded mine and the other being the real goods: a large enterable magnetite iron mine with an impressive adit, so be sure to bring the Big Flashlight along. We'll do plenty of walking on the way there and back. Climbing to high points and negotiating some challenging water crossings keep things from getting dull. Many trials lie ahead in our path.

Starting out on the yellow-blazed trail, we'll follow as it winds through a low swampy area, frequently hopping rocks to cross

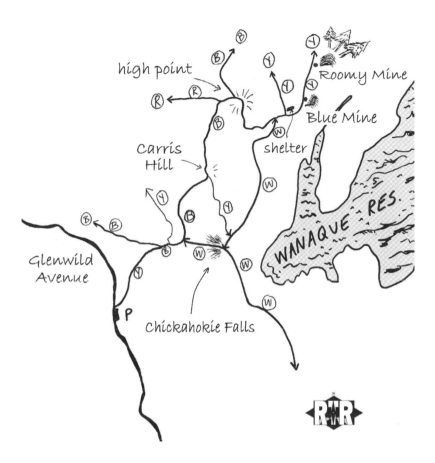

high point

Roomy Mine

Blue Mine

Carris Hill

shelter

Glenwild Avenue

Chickahokie Falls

WANAQUE RES.

P

endless streams. In summer, there is usually no trouble crossing, but rain or spring snow melt in other months can make things complicated. Unless you plan on getting soaked, do another hike in this book in wet weather, and come back here when things dry out.

Yellow climbs to an intersection with the Hewitt Butler Trail (blue-blazed), totally appropriate nomenclature for an iron mine investigation because Abraham Hewitt was an ironmaster in Ringwood during the busy years (and maybe Butler refers to the nearby town?). The Highland Trail, which will someday be a long distance route, joins up and keeps us company for the first half of this hike. Yellow veers off shortly, but blue is what we want. The trail turns sharply to the left (north) at a point where a white trail begins.

Climbing up Carris Hill, starting at about 550 feet and top-
ping out at 1,000, is a long process with a steady ascent. We must
remember to look around when we reach the rocky sides for the
first viewpoints of the trip. When we reach the intersection with the
yellow Carris Trail, we know we've hit the summit. At about 1,000
feet, this point is actually 100 feet higher than the "high point"
we're heading to, but the views aren't as impressive. Continuing
northward, we pass more views and travel through coniferous forest
while we go up and down along the ridge.

Approaching the high point where the blue and red trails come
together, the real climb begins with a short scramble up slick bald
rocks and past scrubby pines. Hot summer days will find us in the
middle of a crowd as we scout out a suitable lunch spot. The Wanaque Reservoir (pronounced "wanakie") is about 800 feet below us,
and the spires of Manhattan are in the distance to the east. We'll rest
here for a little while and enjoy the view before the push to the mines.

After our break, we'll pick up the red Wyanokie Crest Trail on

a steep downhill track
to more water cross-
ings. Take note of the
white trail we pass on
the right—that's the way
back. Soon enough a yel-
low trail joins up. Because
you've done your research
and looked at the Trail
Conference map before
starting out, you know
the mines are along the
yellow Mine Trail, but
beware! The Mine Trail
is a loop, and we want to
continue straight, so don't
make the left.

Trail to high point

Marked rock pointing the way to high point

High point approach

Walking along yellow will bring us past a rundown, uninviting shelter. It's in poor repair at the bottom of the hill, so there isn't any view, as the Harriman shelters have. I can't imagine why anyone would want to stay there. The only good thing about it is that once we see it, we know the Blue Mine is coming up.

The Blue Mine (18 T 0557366, 4545594) sits on a shelf just above Blue Mine Brook, which is crossed by a sturdy wooden bridge. Although flooded, the mine is a worthy objective just because it's so big. It was active sometime in the 1850s, part of the Ringwood group of mines. Flooding was always a problem during the years it was in operation, with several shutdowns taking place while the water was removed. The mine was last worked around 1905. Just to the left of the opening, a concrete pad and block supported the dewatering pump.

About a half-mile down yellow sits the star of our show, the Roomy Mine (18 T 0557512, 4546142). It was opened around 1840, providing magnetite iron ore. On one of my visits, the leader of a Boy Scout troop was sticking magnets on the rocks, to the surprise of the scouts (and, I must confess, to me, also). One of you is looking unhappily at that small opening in front of us and thinking, "That's it? You can't be serious. Is there anything *impressive* about this mine that we're hiking our butts off to see?" All I can say is, "Get your flashlight out."

First shuck off your pack, toss it through the opening, and get ready to crawl. Don't leave it behind while we enter the mine. I bring my pack anytime I enter a mine, even if it's only for a short distance in. Just in case something awful happens, I want my gear with me such as lighter, first aid kit, food, water, and a signal whistle, to name just a few items. I wouldn't be happy if I was stuck somewhere and my pack was just a few feet out of reach or behind a rock fall.

A sign is posted outside of the mine:

CLOSED FROM SEPTEMBER 1 THROUGH APRIL 20
DUE TO BAT HIBERNATION

White Nose Syndrome, a fatal fungal infection responsible for the deaths of millions of bats in the northeast, has also forced closing in recent years.

The low passage going into the mine is about 1.5 feet high. We need to get down in the dirt on our hands and knees to wiggle through. Once in, there is a large room on the other side open to the sky, with the adit proper just in front of us. It's about 6 feet high

Exiting the Roomy Mine

and wide enough for two people to walk side by side for a bit. The rounded tunnel snakes along for 50 or so feet. Bats reside inside and are easy to spot as they huddle inside drill holes and crevices. We can walk to the end and then do something *everyone* does, which is shut off the flashlights and experience absolute darkness.

This particular mine is unusual in that we can enter legally and safely. The only other mines I know of that look like this are on the Copper Mine Trail in the Delaware Water Gap. There are two mines in that group, but sometimes they are closed off and sealed to visitation (thus they aren't mentioned in this book).

The walk back begins when our mine exploration ends. This can easily turn into a six-hour hike, so without wasting too much time, let's head back to the white Lower Trail, taking it westward around the bases of Wyanokie Crest and Carris Hill. Of note along the way is the intersection with the yellow Carris Trail (we saw the top of the trail earlier today) and a T-bone intersection where the white Lower Trail ends. The trail it connects with is also white (the Post Brook Trail), which can be confusing. Bearing to the right (west) puts us onto the Post Brook Trail toward Chickahokie Falls. In times of high water, the challenges begin here.

If it's dry out, we have a forty-minute walk from the falls back to the vehicles. After rain or a snow melt, it could take longer, and I'm telling you there is *no way* to cross a fast-flowing Post Brook and stay dry, because there are no easy rock or tree bridge crossings. When we got caught in this situation one cold December day, the RTR Investigation Team had to take off shoes and socks and cross the first wide frigid stream we came to, reboot, and then tackle the crossing near the falls. That one got both of us soaked, but fortunately the cars weren't far.

The Post Brook Trail ends at the blue Hewitt Butler Trail we started on, and that in turn brings us back the yellow trail. Turning left (south) brings us back to the car after a seriously long day of peak bagging, iron mine hunting, and stream jumping.

20 THE STONE CHAMBERS OF MEAD FARM

WHERE: Kent, NY

WHY: Multiple mysterious stone chambers, balanced rock, Hawk Rock glacial erratic

DIFFICULTY: Moderate; about 4 miles round-trip, with hills on poorly blazed trails

MAP: www.kentcac.info/hikes

UTM COORDINATES: Mead farmhouse: 18 T 0608745, 4592629; Path to lower chamber: 18 T 0609152, 4592452; Lower chamber: 18 T 0609147, 4592537; Hawk Rock: 18 T 0609002, 4591165 (vicinity)

DIRECTIONS: Get to the intersection of Farmers Mills Road (Route 42) and Whangtown Road in Kent, NY. Take Whangtown Road all the way to the end, where there is a small parking area by a gate. Note: You will need a free Department of Environmental Protection permit to park here, obtainable through its website.

Ancient sacred sites, common food storage structures, or colonial constructions? We will see all, some, or none of those things on our hike today, depending on your point of view, as we eagerly seek out no fewer than three stone chambers and add several other uncommon destinations to our barely blazed route as well. You will need your Big Flashlight for proper chamber inspection.

Before we begin, you will need a Department of Environmental Protection permit to legally park here and hike the lands. It is free and easy to acquire: go to the New York City DEP website and look for Watershed Recreation Forms. You can print the permits at home.

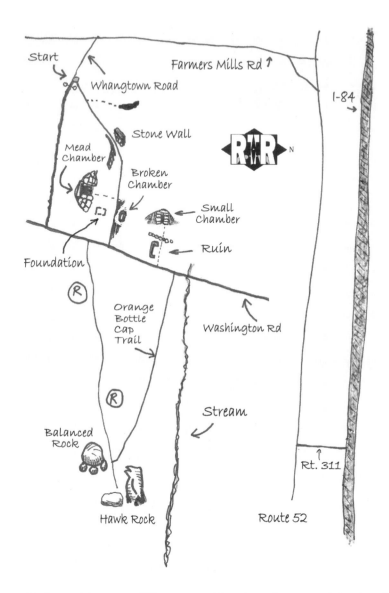

At the parking area, Whangtown Road continues straight ahead, though it's badly deteriorated and gated off. The unblazed footpath we want is to our left, passing a sign for the "Dr. Tom Morgan Preservation Trail." Dr. Morgan was a naturalist involved with the Kent Conservation Advisory Committee, a volunteer organization that advises the town on such issues. It's an unmarked but obvious path that will pass a left-hand spur trail (leading down to a reservoir) a short distance from the start point and then delve into the woods over gentle hills for about a half-mile before coming to the Mead Farm remains.

Moses F. Mead owned and operated this farm sometime in the 1860s, and his contributions regarding this area's "stone chambers" is controversial, but we'll get to that part of the story soon enough. First, as we come into the area we'll encounter a large cut-stone wall on our right, said to be the vestiges of his cow barn. Continuing down the trail, as we keep an eye out to the right, that big stone chamber will presently appear and call out to us to come on over and check it out. After we do that, we can find the minor foundation of a small farmhouse about 20 feet southeast of the chamber, with rubble remains of a chimney at one end and what's left of a stoop near the northwest corner.

This is one of the larger chambers I know of, and it is in good condition. There are two smaller chambers nearby, and after we visit them we can equate, contrast, and talk "stone chamber" as we

Mead chamber

Inside the Mead chamber

compare them to other structures, such as root cellars.

Some people say with confidence that Mead built this particular one, but others disagree, stating with certainty that the chamber predates the farm. Maybe he did build the big one, influenced by the two others in the immediate area? If he built that big stone wall we just encountered, it isn't out of the realm of possibility he's responsible for the chamber as well, because the construction and blocks are similar. Mead was a highway superintendent for a while and had access to the oxen, tools, and crews he'd need to construct such a chamber.

The second, smaller chamber is about 40 yards southeast of this one, across the trail and buried into the hillside. It is facing away from us, but well-worn footpaths will point the way there. The lintel stone is cracked, there is a partial cave-in at the rear, and common sense dictates we should stay out. This chamber goes well into the hillside and is of a rougher construction than the first, also considerably smaller and possibly older as well. The last chamber we'll uncover, down abandoned Washington Road, is of a comparable size to this one but in better condition; we'll see it later on.

Hundreds of these chambers are scattered throughout New England, and several are also found in Westchester and Putnam Counties. Finding them while hiking falls into two distinct categories: easy to locate, such as the big Mead that is right off the trail, or those that are camouflaged and facing away from us, which makes finding them exciting.

Who built them? How old are they? We don't know.

There are no obvious plans or records of these structures being built by colonial settlers, and in fact the chambers appear to precede them. Eastern tribes of Native Americans aren't known to build structures like these. Some certainly appear to be older than others, judging by the weathering of stone and volume of vegetative growth in and around them (including generations of lichens), while some might even qualify as being relatively "new" or built later in the construction period. We don't know, and the clues aren't given up easily.

So what are they for, or to be more exact, what would their original purpose have been? Could they be root cellars? Used for simple storage purposes? Animal pens? Celtic burial chambers? UFO bases or mystical passages to the Andromeda galaxy? Are they built along global ley lines, using the power output from that huge, supernatural earth-energy grid for some unknown purpose? No one can speak with any factual certainty about the subject, because of the lack of substantial proof. It's probable that many of the chambers were altered and repurposed over time to be used as storage areas, root cellars, and so on, making positive use identification or their true age even more challenging.

What do we know about the chambers?

- It is uncertain who built many of them or how old they are.
- Walls are constructed of cut stone blocks using no mortar.
- There are no tool marks on the stones.
- Most have huge, rectangular capstones as roofs, covered over with dirt.
- Some have corbelled (interior-peaked or narrowing) roofs; others are flat.
- There is no apparent provision for a closing door.
- Many are built into hillsides; others are freestanding.
- Some have magnetic material buried at the entrance, altering compass readings.
- Some have carvings at the entrance or other ornamental elements nearby.

- Some have a wide bench along the rear wall.
- Some entrances are oriented toward the south, and a few receive direct solstice light.
- Floors are generally dirt and will frequently pool with water.

Are they root cellars? Root cellars have:
- Ventilated ceilings
- Hinged sets of doors (screened and solid) that can close out the weather, bugs, or animals
- Floors tilted toward the entrance to avoid flooding

Our chambers do not have any of those features.

They were built with a technique similar to the one used in constructing New York City subway lines, employing a "cut and cover" method. The hillside was dug into, and the walls were lined with the stone; once completed, the interior was possibly re-filled, and then the large stones were dragged over them to cover the top. Earth was at times used to conceal much of structure, except for the entranceway. To many people, it appears to be far too much work for the average farmer who only needed a place to put his pigs or corn.

Another question for chamber detectives is: What else besides root cellars do they bring to mind? Pre-Colombian Celtic explorers seem to be the current favorite suspected builders, because the chambers do strongly resemble similar structures called "fougous" (pronounced foo-goos) found in the United Kingdom, often used for burial, defense, or food storage—but as with our chambers, their original purpose has been lost to time. Another similar sort of chamber is a "dolmen," found throughout Europe, Asia, and beyond. Dolmens generally use groups of singular, large, upstanding side stones that are spaced apart (but some have cut-stone sides) and then are capped with sizable top stones.

The chambers themselves are mostly similar from an architectural point of view, and there is a certain "seen one, seen 'em all" aspect to chamber hunting. It's the constructional differences between them that capture our imagination. The question of their origin and appreciation for the significant amount of labor required for their creation is the nexus of our fascination, forming a wonderful mystery to add to our others.

As we finish our inspection of the Mead area, abandoned Washington Road is straight ahead of us. We'll go up to it and then turn right (northwest) for a few yards to an obvious trail heading left (south) into the forest, sometimes indicated with red triangle blazes or red reflectors. That path will reach Hawk Rock in about a mile or so, passing the Balanced Rock as we go. Note a poorly maintained path heading away from the rock at that point.

Hawk Rock, a huge glacial erratic that certainly echoes the shape of an open-beaked hawk with folded wings, will shortly come into view after we pass the Balanced Rock. It's a popular hiking destination, and all kinds of rumors and false assumptions circle around places such as this. Upon close examination, while standing on the large, flat stone just before it, you can see three petroglyphs, a sun, a bird, and a turtle, carved into the breast. Many people suspect these carvings are relatively modern (1920s era), in contrast to those who choose to believe in occult signage or otherworldly origins.

Hawk Rock

After a short break for lunch we'll plot our way back. For the conservative hiker, just turn around and head back to Washington Road on the red trail and await further instructions when you get there. For the daring, back at Balanced Rock we might find the neglected Orange Bottle Cap Trail on our right, marked with deteriorating namesake lids, and do our best to trace on a northwesterly bearing. The lids are only placed on one side of the trees, heading in our direction. If we keep the

Washington Road chamber

stream to our right, we can't get lost and will wind up back on Washington Road.

If you backtracked along the red trail, turn right (north) and head down the road for a quarter-mile to a point where there's a building ruin. If you tried the orange trail and made it, turn left (south) on the road for about 0.2 mile to the same point. Use my "path to lower chamber" UTM coordinates to find it, or just be aware and read the terrain.

At the ruin along the west side of the road, which consists of an edifice shell and some scattered debris, a path will go past the shell and over a low stone wall, quickly leading to our third hillside-buried chamber. Though relatively small and featuring a low entrance that you have to bend down to pass through, this is an older-looking chamber in comparison to some of the others we've come across in our travels and an excellent example of what they look like at their best: primitive, dark, mysterious, slightly menacing.

To return, we'll head back up Washington Road and then backtrack through the Mead site on the same unmarked trail we entered on, examining the big chamber one last time before we go. The ride home can be a good occasion to ruminate on these chambers and recall some others we found while following the "Cranberry Lake Preserve" and "Harriman Ruins in Winter" chapters.

21
SYLVAN GLEN PRESERVE

WHERE: Mohegan Lake/Town of Yorktown, NY

WHY: Extensive quarry operation remains: cut stone blocks, small stone shed, an underpass through granite, cables, foundations, quarrying apparatus, hidden lime kiln

DIFFICULTY: Moderate; roughly 5 miles, with no mountains but lots of up and down on hills

MAP: Sylvan Glen Park Preserve map, available online

DIRECTIONS: Taconic State Parkway to the exit for Bear Mountain Parkway, the next exit after that for Routes 35/202. The road makes a wide, sweeping turn under the Taconic and bears west. Make the first right turn onto Stony Street, and look for the dirt road entrance to the parking lot about 0.4 mile on the left, just before Winding Court.

Sylvan Glen trails bring inquisitive hikers past a huge collection of quarrying apparatus that dates from 1925 through 1941, when the Mohegan Granite Quarry finally closed, as a result of problems that ranged from a lack of manpower caused by World War II to the availability of less expensive building materials. Fortunately for us, much evidence of its operation was left behind for us to see, as opposed to other quarries we have hiked through, such as at Cranberry Lake, where the bulk of the material was removed. Interpretive signs along the way will give a concise history of the place as well as an outline of where the granite eventually was used. Hiking here is both a pleasant nature experience as well as a trip that uncovers the kind of artifacts we love discovering.

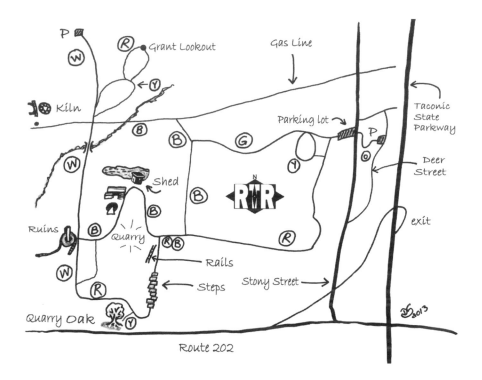

Although there's a more popular parking area on the other side of the park (at the end of Morris Street, near Lexington Avenue), I typically choose to go the less traveled route and pick the "far" lot, and if you're mildly ambitious we can even add a quarter-mile or so (and a minor hill) by parking at the easily found (and better paved) lot off Deer Street. It makes you a better person to choose the more challenging extension at the far lot. (Note: An orange trail at the Deer Street lot leads uphill to join the trail at Stony Street.) Which-ever one we choose, once we find the green trail at the end of the Stony Street parking area, it's easy, level walking on the green Farm Tail to the junction with the blue High Quarry Trail, where a left turn (south) heads toward the heart of the quarry and the "stuff." After a short time, the red Sylvan Glen trail joins in, and the con-joined trails eventually bring us to some huge boulders and rock outcrops. Once we get to the quarrying areas, we'll come across so many pulleys, cables, sheaves, anchoring points, and related objects

Hidden rails

that from here onward it barely makes any sense to point them out. Blue bears right and continues into the working heart of the setup, with some amazing discoveries that we'll explore on the way back.

Continuing on red drops us sharply downhill, and after descending for a brief time it brings us to a point where the massive cut-stone pile on our right narrows down, presenting a footpath that heads to a quarry overlook. Taking the path and looking out over the deep mined valley, on our left (southward) is a short railroad spur, with intact rails and various rusting artifacts scattered about.

Red continues downhill, sometimes on numerous cut stone steps, into the base of the operation, and the unmistakable three hundred- to four hundred-year-old Quarry Oak will soon appear at the end of a short yellow trail. The red trail continues, passing along a stone wall and more of those huge cut blocks, and at the junction of the white Turtle Pond Trail we bear left and in a short while head past foundations and scattered remains of the quarry headquarters. There is a lot to discover at this part of the preserve, both on the trail and off, including remains of buildings, lots of steel cables

Mounting bolt for machinery

Quarry relics

twisting along the path and hanging in trees, plumbing, concrete foundations, unique pulley assemblies lying on the ground, and various kinds of axles and miscellaneous apparatus. Stepping off the trail and heading downhill, westward, offers opportunity to find and photograph numerous bits of odd machinery and plumbing amid the concrete foundations.

White continues through the woods and passes by lots of odd items and a few explanatory placards. When it meets the blue High Quarry Trail, we will take note, because that's the way back. It's white we're staying on for a while as it crosses a wood bridge where plentiful cut stone foundations and cornering mark evidence of past activity along a now-quiet stream.

Soon, white gains elevation and crosses a wide gas pipeline right-of-way that is blue-blazed to the right, uphill, but if we bravely step off-trail and take the unblazed gas line downhill to the left (southwesterly) for about 0.1 mile, we'll discover a quarry-era lime kiln buried into the hillside on the right side of the road, at the base of the hill just before coming to a swampy area. The stone-lined circular burning chamber is easily located by scouting the rise above the lower "arch."

Backtracking to where we left the white trail, turning left (north) and then continuing on, we'll disregard the first yellow blaze we come to and march on for a brief distance to get the other end of that same trail. Picking it up, a lazy figure eight on yellow and then red and then yellow again will pass along more cutting sites and a high point known as the Grant Lookout, where we can pause for a time and choose a good lunch spot.

Properly rested, the hard work is now in front of us. We will retrace the white Turtle Pond Trail to the other end of the blue trail that we ignored (but noted) earlier, now following it to head steeply uphill into the guts of the place. Now, it gets good really fast! The trail follows along the top of a high, steep, dangerous edge, where signs warn us to watch our footing lest we inspect the quarry more quickly heading downward.

So much to find here. Cabling and sheave assemblies, rock eyelet anchors, and more cables bring us up to the most interesting part of the site, where the masons apparently assembled a sort of stone underpass through stacked granite blocks. I've frequently seen rock

Stone underpass

climbers and rappellers on the other side of the valley, ascending and descending the sheer walls of the quarry.

A stone shed by the shore of a pond is another notable feature we'll pass by, and small wildlife likes to congregate here by the water. Though this edifice is identified as a dynamite shed on various websites or in some literature (such as competing hiking books), I have my doubts about that: classic dynamite sheds had thick stone walls and flimsy roofs, designed to direct any accidental explosions upward rather than outward. This shed has thick stone walls as well as a sturdy stone roof and small openings on the sides, looking more like a spring house though there's no evidence any such spring ever existed there. Additionally, one of the interpretive signs we'll notice along the way states that dynamite wasn't used in this quarry because of the way it shattered the granite into unusable shards. I suspect this was a storage building for tools or similar equipment.

This brings us to the end of our quarry investigation, but there's still a little bit of walking to do in front of us. Once the red trial comes into view, we'll part with blue and follow that trail in a serene manner, taking care to bear left (east) as the trail gently roller-coasters up and down to the junction of green, where we bear right, backtracking to the car at whichever lot we left it. A very satisfying hike into quarrying times past, indeed.

22
TWO WORLD'S FAIRS

WHERE: Flushing Meadows–Corona Park, Queens, NY

WHY: Iconic landmarks, optimistic artworks, fair pavilion leftovers, time capsules, two-thousand-year-old column, hidden secrets and mysteries

DIFFICULTY: Easy; level walking (but lots of walking for sure)

MAP: Park map available at Olmstead Center or online

UTM COORDINATES:
Whispering Column of Jerash: 18 T 0597733, 4511270
George Washington Statue: 18 T 0597737, 4511537
Garden of Meditation: 18 T 0597948, 4511025

DIRECTIONS: Grand Central Parkway westbound, to park exit. Head to the lot on the other side of the Queens Museum of Art, closest to the towers.

The 1,255-acre Flushing Meadows–Corona Park in Queens, NY, introduced me to the wonders of photogenic historical leftovers as a young man and is an overlooked gem of a destination for inquisitive vestige hunters such as you and me. It remains my go-to spot for trying out new cameras, and after our exploration today you will understand why that is: between the artifacts we'll discover and the human activity in abundance, there's a lot to shoot. With a good guide on a clear summer day we will uncover some unusual secrets that the park harbors, hidden in plain sight.

Our goal is to time-travel back to the world's fairs that took place here so long ago. Before we begin it's essential to find a map of the old 1964 fairground online and identify the street names from the

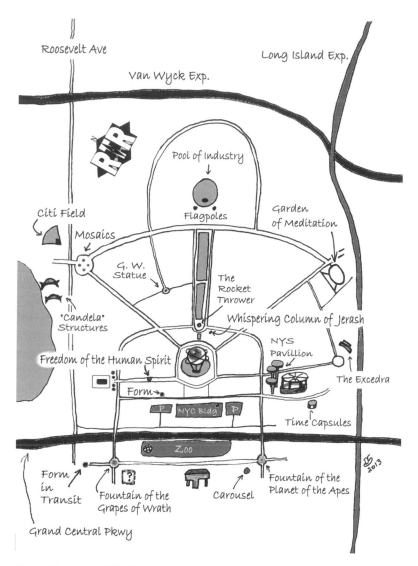

time. Two world's fairs took place in the park, one in 1939–1940
and another in 1964–1965. There are a few remnants from both still
around, waiting for us to discover.

We'll begin at the parking lot just past the Queens Museum of
Art and explore in a generally counterclockwise direction from
there. The famous Unisphere and New York State Pavilion towers

are right there and are an unmistakable beacon that attracts us like moths to flame. It's a definite treat to be here when the fountains are operating around the globe. With a little imagination we can effortlessly step back into 1964 and 1965, the two years that the (sixties) fair ran. Of course we'll take a fast look at the 1939 New York City Building (which houses the Queens Museum of Art) that sits by the lot, and we will certainly get more into that later on in the day.

Right now, the New York State Pavilion's towers sitting along the Avenue of the States are what beckon us to come over to take a look. Skeletal and decaying, they watch over the fair site and are a landmark visible for many miles around, especially from the highways that rim the park. There are three components to the NYSP: the 226-, 181-, and 86-foot observation towers (lowest had a restaurant/lounge), the Tent of Tomorrow, and the Theaterama, now the Queens Theatre and the only part of the complex still in use. A huge mosaic map of New York State graced the floor of the Tent but was damaged in the 1970s when multicolored fiberglass panels were hammered out of the suspension roof above and inexplicably allowed

New York State Pavilion's Tent of Tomorrow

New York State Pavilion's observation towers, 1985

to plummet onto it, beginning a cycle of damage and decay from which the map never recovered. The Tent and Towers are fenced off, tragically abandoned and unused but certainly not forgotten or unloved, and a few proposals for new use are in place but unlikely to be implemented at the present time.

In a quiet grove just SSW of the towers sit the two buried Westinghouse time capsules that are not to be opened until year 6939, five thousand years after the first was interred 50 feet below during the 1939 fair. A squat granite cap from 1965 replaces the original tall marker. There are 305 objects as well as a newsreel in the first capsule and 45 objects in the latter.

Walking around the pavilion will bring us to a popular circular skateboard park, formerly the site of the Astral Fountain. Just past it is a curved stone bench known as The Excedra, commemorating the site of the sizable Vatican Pavilion from 1964. Michelangelo's *Pietà* was displayed there, along with other significant artworks and religious paraphernalia. These days it's used as a changing area and at times a bathroom for athletes using the nearby soccer fields that now lie where the fair exhibits used to be, though religious groups still gather there on occasion.

Heading NNE up the Avenue of Asia to the next major cross street, the Avenue of Africa, we bear right and soon arrive at the entrance to the Garden of Meditation, marked by a sign. Somewhat quizzically situated next to a decidedly unpeaceful spot alongside the Long Island Expressway, a rundown blacktop path meanders through it past seven inscribed inspirational plinths (*n.:* a slablike member beneath the base of a column or pier) and is in a generally neglected (though not abandoned) condition these days. It's one of the few spots left nearly unchanged since the fair days—which only enhances the experience. While we walk through and gaze over at the NYS Pavilion and Unisphere it's suddenly evident that we've achieved our objective: we're at the 1964 New York World's Fair, and it's a bit jarring.

Once our meditative mood has passed, heading to the left (NW) on the Avenue of Africa and then right at the second major cross-road, the Avenue of the United Nations, will bring us past more busy soccer fields and then to the second-oldest outdoor antiquity in New York City (behind Cleopatra's Needle in Central Park), quietly marking time and nearly unnoticed on our left: the Whispering Column of Jerash. An A.D. 120 marble Roman column from a temple to Artemis (the goddess of the hunt) in Jerash, Jordan, it was gifted to New York during the 1964 fair. "Whispering" refers to the way

Whispering Column of Jerash and the Unisphere

voices carried over the inside roof of the temple from one side to the other, similar to the Whispering Gallery in Grand Central Station.

As we're making our way across the park, we also stumble across a few concrete platforms that are left from some fair pavilions. They are in various shapes and mostly inconsequential, but should be noted.

Straight ahead of us is the Unisphere and blue reflecting pools leading from it to the Pool of Industry that contains the white, circular, formerly grand but now-derelict Fountain of the Planets. A well-known photo op is the prominent *Rocket Thrower* statue with the Unisphere behind it, but stick with me—we can find at least one other unusual angle for statue photography in another part of the park. At the head of the pool, close to the Unisphere, are artworks in sandblasted granite panels commemorating both fairs. For now, though, we can follow the pools to the other end, where our first relics from 1939 present themselves: the two ridiculously tall flagpoles topped with art-deco eagles that certainly have an inadvertent Teutonic quality to them.

The next '39 relic is a cast statue of George Washington in full Masonic regalia. Now, I know the pools, statuary, NY State Pavilion, and Unisphere are hard to ignore, much less stop photographing, so instead of continuing on a circuit I'll just pinpoint the location and let you locate it once you're done exploring the vicinity: find the path that bisects the two reflecting pools (east of the *Rocket Thrower*), away from the Unisphere, and follow it straight (northerly) to the statue. Artist Donald DeLue is responsible for both the *George Washington* and *Rocket Thrower* statues. DeLue died in New Jersey at age ninety (1988) and his *New York Times* obituary, in part, read:

> Mr. DeLue was a prolific artist who maintained a career through commissions for large-scale sculptures that, he said, "are intended to last for thousands of years." He made sculptures for Omaha Beach on the Normandy coast of France and for the Federal Court Building in Philadelphia. He created the Boy Scout Memorial Tribute in Washington, the Harvey Firestone Memorial in Akron, Ohio, and "George Washington Kneeling in Prayer" at Valley Forge, Pa.

At this point in our exploring we can find a bench around the statue, surrounded by cherry trees, and take a short break while we ruminate on other aspects of the park. This side of the grounds has much newer structures that postdate the fair by decades: the Arthur Ashe tennis stadium, where the U.S. Open takes place, pitch-putt and mini golf, the very new fitness center, an ice rink, and some dinosaur-themed playgrounds. The Louis Armstrong stadium dates from the '64 fair and was then known as the Singer Bowl. There'd been talk about holding Grand Prix auto races through the park in the 1990s, but thankfully that's never taken place. Another notable new edifice is Citi Field, the stadium that replaced Shea as the home of my N.Y. Mets baseball team. If you walk the stadium's parking lot, you can find plaques inlaid into the asphalt that pinpoint where the bases, pitching mound, and home plate from Shea used to be.

The Olmstead Center is just north of where we are (following the road that parallels the Grand Central Parkway westbound) and is the former administrative offices from the '64 expo, currently serving as the headquarters of the Design, Construction, and Engineering

"Candela Structures" at the Flushing Bay marina

Divisions of Parks. If you can talk your way inside, you may view the architectural drawings of the fair that are mounted on the walls.

Farther north, sitting along a promenade beside Flushing Bay are two (of three) remaining white Fiberglas wave-roofed constructions known as the Candela Structures, after the artist who supposedly designed them (but may not have). They are not bus shelters but rather fair exhibit structures whose outside glass walls and framework have been removed.

At a point almost directly north of us, a ramp by the low Passarelle Building connects the park to Citi Field and the Long Island Railroad and 7 train stations. Restrooms are located there. New artworks in mosaic tile are inlaid into the pavement at this end of the ramp and recall both fairs and Robert Moses, the guiding force behind those fairs and a controversial figure in New York City history. Also in this vicinity are a few inscribed curbstones from the '64 fair, and others are scattered around other sections of the park: Avenue of the Americas, Avenue of Progress and many more; it's a bit of a game trying to find them.

Heading back to the path that runs past the tennis stadium, continuing counterclockwise to a point where four tall flagpoles signal the entrance to the stadium, we reach what is probably my favorite park vista and an absolutely great place to pause while we soak it

Inscribed curbstone

My favorite spot

all in: the *Freedom of the Human Spirit* sculpture with the Towers, Unisphere, and manicured landscaping behind it. Walkers, joggers, and cyclists passing busily by on the paths add a human aspect to a sight that you just do not see anywhere else. It makes me smile (and a little wistful, as well) every time. The sculpture *Form* is on the next path down, in the direction we're heading.

Heading across the North Bridge that spans the Grand Central Parkway puts us on the way to the Hall of Science, significantly expanded since the days of the fair and one of the few exhibits that still exist. The Rocket Park on the other side features authentic 1964-era state-of-the-art space exploration hardware and has been nicely cleaned up following decades of inattention. Another sculpture, *Form in Transit*, sits just down the road.

At this junction, with the Avenue of Transportation, is the circular Fountain of Progress North, but it was renamed Fountain of the Grapes of Wrath sometime in the 1980s by Henry Stern, a New York City Parks Commissioner under Mayor Ed Koch, who had a peculiar sense of humor. Signs with the new designation were regularly stolen (and not by me). There's also the similar Fountain of Progress South farther over by the carousel, renamed Fountain of the Planet of the Apes, which had its own disappearing sign as well. I'd truly hate to get into Mr. Stern's demented head, but here's my theory on his singular method of free association: you have the Fountain of the Planets . . . then the Fountain of the Planet of the Apes . . . then you have the Apes and the Grapes . . . I need to sit down.

I'll sit down at a bench near a wide open area near the fountain and opposite the conspicuous zoo and steel-mesh aviary that rises behind the iron fence. This is the site of the Underground Home, a fancy, plush model bomb shelter from the '64 fair, and I believe it was not removed but buried and might still be here under us. Terrace on the Park next door was a heliport and lounge from the '64 expo and is in the shape of four Ts, for Transportation. It's in use as a catering hall.

The Queens Zoo features North American mammals and post-dates the fair by four years, being an early pioneer in "naturalistic" zoo settings as opposed to animal jails. The dome that we spotted earlier is a Buckminster Fuller design, also from 1964, and it was dismantled and stored for some time before being reused as the aviary. Inside, it has a winding path that can be walked. A petting zoo is across the way.

Not really a ruin but certainly historic, the delightful carousel has original hand-carved horses, lions, dragons, etc. and was combined from two Coney Island rides. My favorite horses are the angry-looking ones.

Finishing up and winding down, crossing back over the South Bridge toward the towers brings us back to the New York City Building, built for the '39 event. The United Nations met there for a time before moving to Manhattan, and it now houses the Queens Museum of Art, which contains the well-known NYC Panorama scale model that's well worth viewing. Way back when I was in grade school both the New York City Building and Hall of Science were regular field trips. I recall in detail the moving, trainlike cars that once circled the model. The skating rink that existed at one end (near us) was removed to enlarge the museum and has been relocated to the Aquatic Center and Ice Rink at the northeastern end of the park.

Our last site, and the most melancholy, is recalled by a plaque on the southern side of the building facing the Unisphere. The plaque reads:

THIS PLAQUE IS DEDICATED TO THE MEMORY OF
DETECTIVES JOSEPH J. LYNCH AND FERDINAND A. SOCHA,
BOMB AND FORGERY SQUAD, WHO WERE KILLED IN THE
LINE OF DUTY WHILE EXAMINING A TIME BOMB TAKEN
FROM THE BRITISH PAVILION OF THE WORLD'S FAIR IN
FLUSHING MEADOW PARK AT 4:45 P.M. ON JULY 4, 1940.

The detectives were examining a ticking satchel that uniformed policemen had removed from the British Pavilion and placed at a cordoned-off spot near the Polish pavilion, where the elevated Van Wyck Expressway now passes over. Dynamite inside went off, killing both of them and wounding many others in the vicinity. No one was ever arrested despite intensive investigations that focused on either American Nazis or IRA sympathizers, and remember, this was before the United States entered World War II.

We've only explored a small section of this huge park. There are two lakes (with a 1939-era boathouse on one of them), Citi Field, and so much more that return visits are not only required but anticipated. The Hall of Science, Panorama, and carousel are very enjoyable places to visit, photograph, or take the kids or a date.

23
WATCHUNG RESERVATION

WHERE: Mountainside, NJ

WHY: Deserted Village of Feltville, two abandoned quarries, Suicide Tower, two mill ruins, copper mine, Magic Forest, historic cemetery, Nike missile base site

DIFFICULTY: Moderate; about 8 miles with relatively minor elevation changes

MAP: Watchung Reservation trail map and Deserted Village of Feltville pamphlet, available at the Trailside Nature Center and elsewhere

CONTACT: Trailside Nature and Science Center, 452 New Providence Road, Mountainside, NJ 07092; phone 908-789-3670

DIRECTIONS: I-78 west to exit 43, New Providence/Berkeley Heights. After the exit ramp merges with Hill Road, make a right at the first traffic light, McMane Avenue, and go straight to where it ends at Glenside Avenue (Route 527). Left on Glenside (note the closed off road that passes over the highway and heads uphill because we'll mention it later in the hike), right on W. R. Tracy Drive (Route 645), and at the traffic circle turn right on Summit Lane. Follow the signs to the Trailside Nature and Science Center.

This is a weird one, folks, so let's get started.

The 2,000-acre Watchung Reservation has a sinister quality that is impossible to ignore. Murder, suicide, a self-styled emperor's autocratic rule, floating limbs, whispers of past satanic rituals and the Cold War all play a part. We'll get into the details as we do our exploration, but to experience the effect to its fullest we must

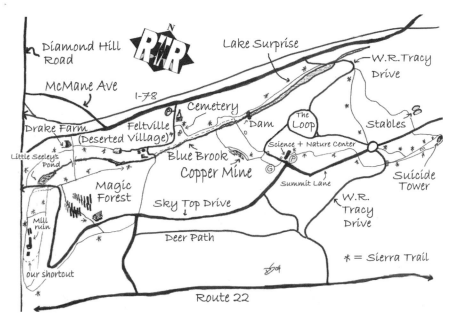

carefully plan the appropriate sort of day for this hike. Sunny summer days full of blooming flora, chirping birds, and playing children just won't do; instead we'll pick a gloomy day near the end of winter, when the newer pines are enshrouded by a low gray fog, a hint of rain is in the air, and the older deciduous trees gently wave their bare branches at us through the mist in mute warning of the real and imagined horrors that await us just down the trail.

Even the name Watchung has a vaguely ominous sound, a sort of comic-book sound effect of axe hitting bone. In reality, it comes from the Lenape word for "high hills," a reference to the topography north of the park.

The local deer population, whose numbers have grown too quickly for their own good, have reason for their own instinctive concern. As I drove to the trailhead, I spotted a few that met a sudden end via auto on the side of the road. To control the exploding numbers, the county has controversially authorized seasonal culls under police supervision. Signs are conspicuously posted when the culling is in session, warning careless hikers to stay on the trails and resist bushwhacking. On the trail or not, gunfire is not something you ever want to hear while hiking.

For purposes of navigation, we have to recognize the difference between bridle trails (solid lines) and footpaths (dotted lines) as indicated on the park map. Be advised that this park has a reputation for changing trail colors. It's also worth noting that many of the trails are often very muddy throughout the park, so waterproof footwear is essential for ensuring success and dry socks.

Our adventure begins at the Trailside Nature and Science Center. We'll start early in the morning, so we can finish up during its operating hours (daily, 12–5 P.M.) for a quick visit before the ride home.

The white-square-blazed Sierra Trail is the main trail in this park, forming a 10.5-mile loop as it goes along, frequently conjoining with other blazed trails. Following the Sierra Trail from the Nature and Science Center in a northwesterly direction will soon lead us past our first site, an old copper mine dug out of a brook running through a deep ravine. The broken rock littering the area clearly reflects the patina of oxidized copper, though most of it is worthless basalt. It is believed that this mine was merely a test dig sometime in the 1700s, predating the other endeavors we'll soon uncover. The mud, sometimes ankle-deep, relentlessly sucks at our waterproof hiking boots as we pass through.

We're now heading downhill as a blue trail joins the Sierra. Soon we'll see the slow-moving, shallow Blue Brook ahead of us. The brook is an outflow of Lake Surprise, which was dammed at the western end in the mid-1800s to provide power for David Felt's paper mill.

We'll leave the Sierra for a bit and follow Blue Brook to the west. At the point where the next bridle trail connects at a bridge, if we cross over we can inspect the slim remains of David Felt's paper mill along the brook. We'll find out a little more about that enterprise a bit later in the afternoon when we explore the Deserted Village. Cross over the bridge again and follow the bridal path uphill, eventually passing a group of private homes on our left. The lights from these homes, shining coldly through the trees, have undoubtedly stirred the imaginations of young adults looking for a scare as they explore the park after hours, because they're visible for quite a distance in subdued light.

Bearing directly south (left), we'll follow the bridle trail as it crosses Sky Top Drive and then heads in a southwesterly direction for a quarter-mile (from the road) to another junction with the Sierra Trail. Following the white squares, we cross the road once again and come to the Sky Top Picnic Area.

A major advantage to taking this hike out of season or during the week is that this usually busy place is hushed and empty. Noisy crowds will just destroy the mood we're working so hard to create! A covered area with some picnic tables, the inside roof strangely painted in a sort of camouflage, might shield us from the drizzle for a while as we consider the dense woods a few yards past the protection of the shelter. Let's take a short break here before journeying up the trail into the enigmatic Magic Forest.

It's known to area residents as either the Enchanted Forest or the Magic Forest, but whatever it's called, this is one unusual place. Actually a pine plantation courtesy of the Civilian Conservation Corps in 1927, the area features sixteen thousand pine trees planted in endless ruler-straight rows, with all the trees inside being the exact same distance apart from each other. When you hear whispers of furtive late-night rituals or Satan worship in the Watchung Reservation, this is ground zero. Downed trees and dead stumps

Magic Forest

seem to echo the suspicion that robed figures are loitering in the
shadows, just waiting for us to leave so they can continue their
evil rites. Park personnel and the Mountainside Police have told
me there is no basis to these stories. The mysterious lights that are
sometimes seen flickering down the paths after dark are from the
private homes nearby, just outside of the reservation.

Although the white-square blazes head straight down one
of the rows, it's absolutely impossible to stay on the trail. The
pines are all the same height and circumference, and all have tall,
straight trunks that are completely barren of low branches. You
wander off, photographing the weird patterns that the rows create, looking up at the sky (if we're unfortunate enough to be here
on a nice day) through the trees, wondering about all those fallen
pines that break up the monotony of the straight rows, and then
you suddenly realize that you can't find the trail! The ground is
absolutely flat, and all the rows look alike. Getting one's bear-
ings or finding a point of reference is nearly impossible. That old
uncomfortable feeling of not knowing where you are takes hold.
It begins with unease and then quickly graduates to serious concern. Am I really lost? Where's the trail? Was someone looking at
me through the trees?

Getting back on the trail successfully when you've lost the way
is what separates the experts from the amateurs in the hike leader
game, so naturally we're soon back on track, heading north through
this strange artificial forest. At the next bridle trail junction, the
Sierra turns to the right (east) but we're going to the left (west). At
0.2 mile, the trail crosses Sky Top Drive at a parking area next to
Little Seeley's Pond, and there's the Sierra again on the other side
of the road.

We aren't taking it. Instead, we'll pick up the footpath that follows Blue Brook, eventually passing a dam and a series of smaller
cascades downstream. To no one's surprise, the Sierra again
appears, goes up and over an escarpment and then delivers us to an
impressive home foundation with a brick pillar next to it, presumably from a gate. A mill foundation is just down the trail, as is a
rock cut that fed water to the mill. The park naturalist told me this
might be a natural formation, considering the fact there are no tool

or blast marks in the rock, but I disagree. We've walked through too many man-made cuts on these explorations not to notice one when our feet are upon it.

There are plenty of interesting artifacts at this mill site to uncover as we rummage around. The only thing dampening our cautious enthusiasm is the traffic noise from New Providence Road on the other side of the brook. There is what appears to be a steam boiler buried along the path near the old mill. The hillside to our left is loaded with broken rock from an old quarry.

As we approach the end of the escarpment, to our left an old road appears, presumably from the mill operation days. Turning left (southeasterly), we'll save a few steps by taking the old road up to a fire ring, where we'll then see the trail just above us. We again bear left (northerly) and follow the Sierra back to Sky Top Drive. That little shortcut saved us about fifteen minutes of walking and spared us the indignity of hiking past a noisy rock quarry operation and construction site.

For the next two or three miles we're sticking with the Sierra Trail, so after a short rest our hike continues. The trail bears left (west) at Sky Top Drive and then goes sharply to the right into the woods. After crossing a boardwalk, the Sierra makes a left on a foot trail and then turns right in short order, but we aren't going right just yet. If we continue straight past the Sierra junction on the path, the 1940s-era Drake Farm site appears on the left side of the trail, consisting of a brambly rock-lined foundation. Not much is known about the history of the site, so after we're done snooping around (looking for a spring somewhere in the vicinity) we'll continue through the gloom on white for 0.6 mile to the major historic site in this park, the Deserted Village of Feltville.

Some of my information on Feltville comes from the park's self-touring pamphlet. Feltville (known in later years as Glenside Park) has had many different incarnations since the 1700s. It was a farming community, a mill town under David Felt, a lonely group of deserted homes, and for a short time renewed life as a summer resort. It's also been a late-night destination of bored teens looking for a scare, thus getting them involved in all sorts of mischief. This isn't a ghost town by any stretch of the imagination. Today, some of the buildings have been renovated for private use, while others are awaiting proper attention.

The first settler in the vicinity was Peter Willcocks from Long Island. After damming Blue Brook he built a sawmill, selling the products to other settlers. Once the land was cleared, his family and descendants farmed the area for the next hundred or so years.

Enter David Felt in 1844. A manufacturer of stationery from New York City, he started buying land from the Willcocks family with the intention of building another paper factory to supply his store. (He already had one factory in Brooklyn.) From 1845 to 1847 he built the factory, put his own dam on Blue Brook to supply the power, and raised the town that housed his workers. His village became known as Feltville. Mr. Felt set himself up as an emperor of sorts, becoming known as King David. Residents were required to attend Sunday services at the big house up the trail, which doubled as the town store. The townspeople could buy produce he grew and meat from his livestock at the store, and there was even a post office inside. A one-room schoolhouse stood up the road where the parking lot is today.

The first structure we come to is the Masker's Barn, an 1882 structure from the Glenside Park era used to store carriages and horses that were used to transport residents to the train station in Murray Hill. There is presently some renovation under way. Just up the road are three small Feltville homes that may have been used by childless couples working in the mill. Passing the third home, the road downhill goes to the mill ruin we walked by earlier today.

Staying on the main road, four more cottages in various states of disrepair come into view. The orange plastic fencing prevents us from close inspection and unfortunately, it seems to get in the way when we take our cameras out. There were four other buildings on this block that have been either burned down or removed, for a total of three buildings in the front row and five in the back. By 1850, there were a total of about 175 people living in these buildings. All the buildings were divided in half by a common chimney and wall, with separate entrances and staircases in each section.

Continuing up the road, the store/church building comes into view. Resist the urge to check out the path to the cemetery. A small welcome center is on the ground floor of the big building and is

Feltville cabins

Feltville cemetery

open during the summer. The Adirondack porch and steeple were added to the building in the later Glenside Park years.

The little town survived Felt's rule until 1860, when it was sold to Amasa Foster. The former emperor then returned to New York City, possibly because of his brother Willard's poor health. Upon leaving his kingdom, Felt is reported to have said, "Well, King David is dead and the Village will go to hell!" The property changed hands six times over the next twenty years, with some businesses manufacturing cigars, silk, or sarsaparilla, but none were successful. By late 1880, the town was known as the Deserted Village. King David's prediction had come true.

Feltville was bought in 1882 by Warren Ackerman, who converted the property into a summer resort and renamed it Glenside Park. All the buildings were renovated and some, like the store/church, were given Adirondack accents. Dormers were added to the larger cottages to make the second floor more livable. The improvements gave each old building some new life and a unique personality.

Glenside Park offered its residents golf, croquet, tennis, baseball, fishing, and horseback riding until 1916, when times changed and the automobile allowed people to travel further into the country. Glenside Park, like Feltville, began to fade into a deserted village again. In 1920, the property joined the Watchung Reservation, and the houses were again rented in the 1960s. While it's far from deserted, the Deserted Village is still a distinctive feature of the park and well worth a visit.

One more site to visit that's related to the village lies just ahead on the Sierra, and that is the historic cemetery on the hill behind town. We can take the signed path up to the site. On close inspection, it seems there is a remarkable mystery here: John Willcocks has two tombstones next to each other. One is an original, but what's up with the new one? They're both for the same person, the son of original settler Peter. The newer tombstone is from an effort by the Daughters of the American Revolution to properly identify some residents of the cemetery who served in the military. None of these stones are standing on the actual grave site, and it's possible that there are up to twenty-four people buried here. It makes us uneasy thinking that we might be standing on someone.

Many footpaths spider-web away from the cemetery, but naturally it's the Sierra that we want. The trail continues along for 1.3
flat, muddy miles. Interstate noise occasionally intrudes as we pass
by a quarry, a Boy Scout campsite, and the dam for Lake Surprise.
It's a fact that body parts were found floating in the lake during
the early 1970s (and some more were found in a garbage bag fairly
recently.) The '70s was a grim decade for this park.

When the Sierra crosses W. R. Tracy Drive at the end of Lake
Surprise, we have some careful navigation to do. Following the
Sierra around a wood fence, we'll bear to the right and then left as
we follow a horse trail in a southeasterly bearing. The Watchung
Stables and riding rings soon appear before us.

What is so interesting about some active stables? The buildings
sit upon the launcher sites where the Army and National Guard
operated Nike Ajax and Hercules missiles from 1957 to 1963. Nikes
were the last of the ground-based antiaircraft defense systems. The
control site (radar antennas and manned buildings) was located next
to present-day Governor Livingston Regional High School, on top
of that closed road off Glenside Avenue that we passed earlier this
morning. No trace of either Nike site is visible today, but I'd be neg-
ligent in my responsibility if I allowed us to ignore the historical
significance of the place. It's just another aspect of the deadly serious business we've come to expect from the Watchung Reservation.

The deadliest is quickly approaching. Following the entrance
road for the stables brings us to Summit Lane, where we bear right
for a few yards before turning left on a footpath. We know what's
coming up. A slight feeling of foreboding increases as we trek
through the misty woods on our approach to the Suicide Tower.

Slowly revealed through the bare branches as we advance, the
150-foot-high water tower rises up before us like a giant tombstone,
its top disappearing into the fog. Once we learn the structure's grue-
some history, it becomes even more powerful and awesome.

There had been at least two suicides from the tower summit
before the night of Tuesday, January 15, 1975. On that day, fif-
teen-year-old Gregg Sanders, a sophomore at the private Pingry
School in Hillside, came home from school at about 4:45 P.M. By
most accounts he was a good student from a fine family and gave no

Suicide Tower

indication to his teachers or school staff of any unusual home or school problems he might be having. Or maybe they just weren't paying enough attention.

Gregg was harboring a bleak secret that was about to come to light. The Mountainside Police told me he hadn't slept for a week, possibly fueled by the drugs that his sister, a nineteen-year-old college student in Massachusetts, had been mailing him. He had written a note to "Whom It Concern" prior to that day's event, and placed it under a paperweight on his desk. The note detailed exactly what was on his mind and what he intended to do.

His father, Thomas Sanders Jr., forty-eight, was an executive with First National City Bank. He was sitting at the kitchen table going over some bank paperwork when Gregg hit him several times in the back of the head with a 2-foot axe. Gregg then struck his nightgown-clad mother Janice, forty-four, once in the head when she came downstairs to see what all the noise was about.

Sanders then ran out of the house wearing only a T-shirt and khaki pants. Watchung Reservation was less than a mile from their home. The tall water tower at the eastern end was a popular spot after dark for youthful adults to see the lights of New York City or have some privacy. He headed to the water tower, climbed the cold steel stairs to the top, and then leaped out into the January night after slitting his left wrist.

Four young visitors looking for a late-night diversion discovered Gregg's body at about 11:15 P.M. While attempting to notify his parents later that night, police discovered their butchered bodies and the bloody axe when they entered an unlocked rear door of the home because there was no response to phone calls or knocking. The suicide note in the upstairs bedroom stated that Gregg murdered his parents because he did not want them to live with the knowledge he had killed himself. He killed them as an act of love.

The true motivation for the crime remains a mystery, though there is some documentation that Gregg endured some teasing from his schoolmates because he wasn't as good a student as his older sister was. How is it possible that no one at Pingry School or even his doomed parents took note that he hadn't slept for so long? He obviously had been living with this intention for a long period of time. Why didn't any of his close friends or schoolmates pick up on this? Did they keep it to themselves?

The tower steps were removed soon afterward at the insistence of the local PTA. The Pingry School has relocated. Gregg's sister lives in Connecticut, last anyone heard. The story made the *New York Times* and national headlines. It rose to local myth and is still subject to much embellishment and retelling. While many of the stories about horrible midnight activities in Watchung Reservation may indeed be just stories, this one is an unsettling fact.

The image of that indifferent steel tower rising up from its high point like some monstrous cenotaph is hard to shake, and it stays with us even after we have left it and are back on the path. We all look back at it over our shoulders more than once. Heading back on the Sierra (by the trail, not the bridle path) toward the Nature and Science Center, there is a sense of remorse that will remain with us after the hike is done.

We won't end things this way. There is one trick left up my damp sleeve. Returning to our cars outside of the nature center, we'll drop our packs and go inside. This bright, cheerful, and airy building replaces the previous dreary old dark one that wasn't much fun and struck us as being downright eerie!

Stepping back outside into the cold air, we reflect on this insane outing. The Magic Forest, Lake Surprise with its floating body parts, the Deserted Village, and Suicide Tower are all appropriate objectives for a long hike on a rainy day.

24
WEST POINT FOUNDRY

WHERE: Cold Spring, NY

WHY: Extensive foundry ruins

DIFFICULTY: Easy; all trails total about 3 miles, with hills

MAP: Online or at kiosk

WEBSITE: www.westpointfoundry.org

CONTACT: Putnam History Museum, 63 Chestnut Street, Cold Spring, NY 10516; phone 845-265-4010

DIRECTIONS: Taconic State Parkway to Route 301 west. Continue west on Main Street in Cold Spring (toward the Hudson River), bear left on Rock Street, then right on Kemble Avenue (Gouverneur Kemble was a founder of the West Point Foundry), following signs to the preserve. Restrooms are near the parking lot.

The West Point Foundry Preserve site has certainly seen its share of change over the years, progressing from noise, industry, and pollution to now peaceful parkland where we can spend a decent morning or afternoon wandering amid some fine ruins. It pays to check the website first and find the page that interprets the numbered points of interest we'll find along the way. There's an audiovisual tour that augments this map, so you can follow a narrated tour through the cleaned-up, but still ruinous, foundry. A pamphlet with a map (but no numbered points) is available at the information board at the start of the trail.

This is an excellent, easy trail for families with young hikers. The trails are all easy to find and follow, leading to many points of interest.

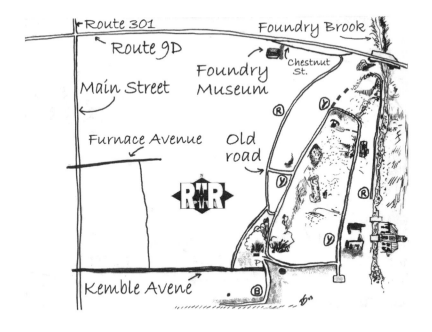

The foundry was built in the 1820s, primarily for the construction of ordnance, but it also manufactured locomotives, engines, and machine parts. During the Civil War years, West Point Foundry hit its peak. Foundry superintendent Robert Parrott had perfected a rifled cannon that was powerful, accurate, and locally produced, and the supply couldn't keep up with the demand! The foundry used huge amounts of natural resources, such as locally mined iron ore, water, and trees for the furnace. After the war, peacetime and the lack of demand for fresh cannon began the foundry's decline; by 1920 parts of the property were being leased to other companies. Nickel cadmium batteries were produced as late as 1970. In later years, Foundry Cove was a Superfund federal cleanup site as a result of the massive amounts of heavy metal dumping that took place over the manufacturing years. Partnering with Michigan Tech, the environmental organization and land trust Scenic Hudson has recently (2013) improved the trail system and interpreted the site after an extensive archeological study. There are many explanatory signs at key points of interest as we travel around the area.

Foundry office

Ruined foundry wall

Near the parking lot, the yellow trail splits: the left leg heads uphill in a roughly northerly direction while the right leg heads east, passing an information board, and follows marshland to the replica

Shop building ruins

of a gun-testing platform that overlooks the marsh. The trail continues on past a few intriguing, overgrown building shells that we
need to scrutinize. At press time, the plastic-wrapped cupola has
been removed from the roof of the office building and set aside for a
renovation that no one has yet scheduled.

The shuttered foundry office building is the most notable ruin
down here, and thankfully, it's in reasonably good condition. The
office was erected in 1865, a time when the Civil War was over and
the once-booming foundry was beginning to come upon bad finan-
cial fortunes. The two-story structure stands in faded glory along
lively Foundry Brook, occasionally open to visitors at various times
during the year.

The red trail begins near a picnic area and follows Foundry
Brook northerly while bypassing the indications of many old, now-
gone structures: foundations, whatever hardware is still sticking up
through the soil, and plenty of slag. Slag is everywhere. It looks
like gray volcanic rock, but is really light, porous waste from the
iron-making process. The red blazes end just before the recently
excavated blast furnace ruin that perches on a mound not far from
the underside of the Route 9D bridge. We can carefully climb the

Foundry furnace

mound and check out the half-buried furnace arch, then turn around and pick up the yellow trail.

Standing at the top of the hill, looking south, we have our back to the furnace and see, in order, the battery pond, blacksmith shop site below us, and the waterwheel area conspicuous on the right, with the office building at the end of the end of the trail. At this point the yellow trail goes straight down the middle of the manufacturing area but also turns right (west) and heads up the steps to follow a rail bed that gives good high views of the area. We'll have to do both paths as we explore, finishing up on the "upper" yellow trail where it intersects with red (there are two junctions, either will work).

An option for our tour would be to coincide our walk with a time when the Putnam History Museum, the former school for foundry workers' children, is open (call for hours). We can follow the red trail up to Chestnut Street, where we'll turn left and find the museum. On display are rotating exhibits on local history and a room dedicated to the foundry, along with some items that were manufactured here. This is a very worthwhile place to stop by.

After visiting the museum, we'll retrace and head back to the parking lot on the red trail, but there's still a little more to do before we're done. The blue trail follows marshland as it heads toward Cold Spring's waterfront and train station; along the way, it also passes the vacant Kemble House and a historic chapel on the Hudson riverside. Cold Spring's main street is lively and has many shopping and dining opportunities.

APPENDIX Places That Aren't Mentioned in This Book

MINE HILL PRESERVE, ROXBURY, CT

A 5-mile trail loop passes by a furnace complex and some bat-caged mines, making for an excellent day of exploration in neglected (by me) western Connecticut.

The furnace at Mine Hill

CAMP GLEN GRAY, MAHWAH, NJ

This former Boy Scout property is now county-run and has inexpensive primitive camping very close to the metropolitan area. It is easily accessible by public transportation from New York City via NJ Transit rail to Suffern and then a short taxi ride from the train station. Hiking trails lead right from your campsite (pick the Augie Schroeder memorial site) to mountaintop panoramic views and two abandoned scout camps in the area, Camp Tamarack and Camp Todd (with limited standing remains at either place), as well as a nearby trail abounding with semi-finished millstones. Write-ups detailing the various historic hikes are available at the office.

Camp Glen Gray millstone

JUNGLE HABITAT, WEST MILFORD, NJ

The ruins of this former drive-through animal park are available for exploration off Route 511, not too far away from Long Pond Ironworks State Park in Ringwood. To get there, find Greenwood Lake Airport. As you're heading to the airport, you'll see the unmistakable entrance to the park on the left.

Keep going to the massive 3,000-car parking lot, where you'll find twin tunnels that lead into the walk-through section.

Warner Brothers ran Jungle Habitat for about four years during the mid-1970s. Damage to cars on the drive-through and reported mistreatment of the animals eventually led to closure of the place. The property was recently added to Norvin Green State Park, allowing legal exploration of the site.

I haven't added it to the book because, although it is lawful to enter, there is a confusing maze of unblazed paved trails that snake around both the walk-through and drive-through sections. I couldn't possibly lead you through in print, but if you have the time and a GPS, it is a worthy place to visit. You can bike the drive-through part . . . if you can find it.

Taylor Steelworkers Historical Greenway

TAYLOR STEELWORKERS HISTORICAL GREENWAY, HIGH BRIDGE, NJ

Many historic sites and ruins are on this hike, but following the trail is the hard part—it's poorly marked, if at all. Highlights of the exploration include the TISCO historic site, Solitary House grounds (don't miss the slave quarters—bring your ghost hunting gear), and the Springside farm ruin at the end of the trail.

VAN SLYKE CASTLE, RAMAPO MOUNTAIN STATE FOREST, NJ

The photogenic ruin of Foxcroft Mansion, also known as Van Slyke Castle, overlooks Ramapo Lake and lies along the white Castle Trail accessed via the upper parking lot off Skyline Drive. The old mansion's water tower is a short distance down the trail and usually enterable. A stone lookout tower, on private property and not enterable, is readily visible from the site. It is south of Camp Glen Gray (not mentioned here as well) and would make a lengthy day hike from your campsite if you stayed there.

FRANNY REESE STATE PARK AND WALKWAY OVER THE HUDSON, POUGHKEEPSIE, NY

You can do a less than 5-mile round-trip over the former railroad bridge, heading to some ruins in the state park across the Hudson River. It is similar in some ways to the High Line in New York City, another repurposed former railway.

MUTTONTOWN PRESERVE, SYOSSET, NY

Estate ruins, a walled garden, and confusing trails on Long Island.

OSCAWANNA PRESERVE, CROTON, NY

The old McAndrews Estate is a very good place to spend a few hours of quality exploration. Wandering around the old estate, you will encounter ruins, an abandoned racetrack, a fountain, and a sense that there's a lot more just out of sight. There are no reliable, maintained, marked trails of any real length on site.

Oscawanna racetrack

Oscawanna fountain

Rock Pond Mine

ROCK POND MINE, TICONDEROGA, NY

An Adirondack graphite mine and quarry with terraced stone foundations and a large boiler, accessed via an easy hike from Putnam Pond State Park campground.

STORM KING MOUNTAIN, CORNWALL, NY

Ruins, walls, and foundations of the 1840s-era Pagenstechter Estate sit way up high on the north side of the mountain, with a smaller

Mark shows me the ruins on Storm King

doctor's home foundation on the south side. The summit offers commanding views of the Hudson River, as well as the sunken barge *Armistead* that sits along the shore below the mountain.

WILLIAM C. WHITNEY WILDERNESS AREA, REGAN POINT, LONG LAKE, NY

This isn't a hike at all but an adventure of an entirely different sort. The spotty remains of a private, miniature "great camp" can be reached by kayak or canoe if you drive up to the Adirondacks and head toward Little Tupper Lake, 7 miles west of Long Lake. Once at the lake, paddle a mile or so across to campsite #7 and marvel at the remains of the pocket-sized "Great Camp" that used to be extant at Regan Point.

The entire vicinity is known as the William C. Whitney Wilderness Area (phone 518-624-6686), after the gentleman who owned it before the state took over. Whitney established "great" Camp Bliss at the western end of the lake sometime around 1923. Nothing remains at the site, but it is still a popular paddling destination.

A Mr. Regan was secretary to Mr. Whitney, and he gained permission sometime in the 1920s or 1930s to build his own, much smaller version of a Great Camp at what is now called Regan Point. There are some stone pillars in the water as you approach. Two lonely fireplaces are attached to the ruins of what must have been fun buildings to party in. There might be more artifacts awaiting discovery if you poke around and look in the corners. The best part is that you can camp there for free, overlooking the magnificent (motor-free) lake. At night, the ruins silhouette against the stars as the loons' otherworldly cries carry eerily across the water.

ACKNOWLEDGMENTS

Thumbs up to the intrepid Road to Ruins Investigation Team: Todd Rutt, Marcus Lieberman, Kevin "The Pit" Zietz, and my son, Noah, who freely and of their own will (except in Noah's case) spent many days and weekends with me, hiking and camping in some odd places.

Mark Jelley for his help with the Doodletown chapter (www. Doodletown.us) and for showing me many amazing sites since we've first met. His knowledge of abandoned Hudson Valley places and their histories is unparalleled. Though Mark has been photographed participating in RTR investigations, he is considered more of a consulting specialist rather than rank-and-file operative.

Renée Fleury (www.kelticenergy.org) for bringing me to some outstanding stone chambers in Putnam County.

David Ehnebuske (www.KentCAC.info) for input on the Mead Farm chapter.

Miner Dan Lopez, Miner Bob Mykytka, and the Abandoned Mines (ABM) crew for inviting me to participate in some astounding underground inspections. Check my posts on the "Abandoned and Neglected" discussion forum at www.abandonedmines.net.

Taro Ietaka for explorations at Cranberry Lake Preserve that forced rewrite after rewrite. *Thanks,* Taro . . .

Jane Daniels for guidance at Sylvan Glen Preserve.

David Lynch of Intelics.com for creating and administering the RTR website.

Shelley Fyman for early edits and writing advice.

Dave Rabin for giving me my first hike leader job.

Iron Mine Trails by Ed Lenik (New York–New Jersey Trail Conference), and *Vanishing Ironworks of the Ramapos* by James Ransom (Rutgers University Press) are two valuable resources for historic mine hunting.

A solemn nod is given to the memories of Douglas Legg and Gregg Sanders, whose sad stories are recounted herein.

To the way-underground IMF Photo Team ("The Impossible Mission Fotographers: Trespassing since 1987") of urban explorers: how does the sunlight feel?

Maps and photos are by the author, unless otherwise indicated.

ABOUT THE AUTHOR

David A. Steinberg is married, has a son, and lives in Westchester County, NY. Over many years he has planned and led hikes and tours for several different organizations. Using photography as an excuse, he continuously attempts to satisfy a longtime fascination with ruins, ghost towns, and similarly abandoned places.

Hiking the Road to Ruins features some favorite New York City–area destinations, collecting years of dedicated exploration into one volume.